Museums of Atlanta

Westholme Museum Guides

Museums of Atlanta

Museums of Boston

Museums of Chicago

Museums of Los Angeles

Museums of New York City

Museums of Philadelphia

Museums of San Francisco

Museums of Washington, DC

Visiting museums is one of the best ways to get to know a city.
Westholme Museum Guides, designed for both residents and visitors,
are the first-ever uniform compilations of permanent collections open
to the public in America's major cities. Each city has its own unique
group of museums, some famous, others practically unknown, but all
of them are important parts of our nation's cultural life.

Museums of Atlanta

A Guide for Residents and Visitors

Scott W. Hawley & Kevin L. Crow

WESTHOLME
Yardley

Acknowledgments
We would like to thank the many curators and staff who were so helpful in researching and preparing this book. Thanks also to the patience of our wives, the guidance of Professor Doug Bowman, the editing skills of Owen and Valerie Davis, and the copy editing of Christine Liddie.

Published by Westholme Publishing, LLC, Eight Harvey Avenue, Yardley, Pennsylvania 19067.

Maps by Joseph John Clark

10 9 8 7 6 5 4 3 2 1
First Printing

ISBN 10: 1-59416-028-7

ISBN 13: 978-159416-028-8

www.westholmepublishing.com

Printed in the United States of America on acid-free paper.

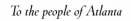

To the people of Atlanta

Contents

Introduction

Originally founded in 1837 as Terminus, a stopover on a sleepy rail line cut through northern Georgia, the town that would become Atlanta has been growing ever since. Today Atlanta is one of the world's most dynamic cities, cementing its place on the global stage by hosting the Olympic Games in 1996. Chic yet folksy, Atlanta is the home to everything from the Jimmy Carter Presidential Library to the nation's premier historically black colleges. And as the headquarters for CNN, Coca-Cola, and Home Depot, the city functions as the business capital of the southeastern United States.

With the recent opening in Atlanta of the Georgia Aquarium — the world's largest with over eight million gallons of freshwater and saltwater exhibits — the city's future is bright. Its past, however, is not without controversy. The land upon which Atlanta was built became available to white settlers only after the United States Congress passed the Indian Removal Act of 1830. The simultaneous discovery of gold in the north Georgia town of Dahlonega, located 65 miles north of Atlanta, hastened the removal of the Cherokees and the Creeks who had called Georgia home for thousands of years. As white settlers streamed into the area, Terminus grew exponentially.

After a second name change to Marthasville in 1843, the bustling town became known as Atlanta by an act of the Georgia Assembly in 1845.

While the city's first citizens struggled to find a name that stuck, very few Georgians believed this railroad junction connecting the state to both Tennessee and South Carolina would ever become more than a depot town. And there was little practical reason to believe it, as most major cities during the 1800s were supplied through a major waterway. Although the Chattahoochee River supported the city's milling industry, it was hardly big enough to support the movement of large trade. However, over time, with the help of the Western & Atlantic Railroad, Atlanta became the gateway to the antebellum South.

Today it is difficult for visitors to experience Atlanta's storied past by simply walking or driving through the city. On the surface, it appears that billions of dollars of recent development has destroyed any semblance of cohesive history. Upon further inspection, however, the answer to this puzzling phenomenon lies in Atlanta's enduring legacy: its incredible ability to change with the times. Over the last 170 years, the people of Atlanta have bravely reinvented themselves, which has transformed the city into a world-class destination. From the Old South to post–Civil War reconstruction, from segregation to assimilation, and from rural backwater to commercial juggernaut, Atlanta has changed in remarkable ways. But with each new reinvention, it becomes more and more difficult to remember what Atlanta was and how it became the magnificent city of today.

Researching and writing *Museums of Atlanta* offered the opportunity to share a thorough understanding of the city's history and heritage and the landmarks and collections that represent them, not only to native Atlantans but also to all who visit here. To that end, this book details many of the city's nationally recognized museums, such as the High Museum of Art and Fernbank Science Center, but it also focuses on lesser-known treasures such as the Wren's House Museum and Oakland Cemetery. We invite you to use this book to embark on your own Atlanta adventure accompanied by family and friends.

Upon traveling to the destinations described in this book, you will quickly notice that Atlanta has proven its early detractors wrong. The railroads that once helped thrust Atlanta into the spotlight left a permanent mark on the city. Atlanta literally grew up around the tracks that served as the core and lifeblood of the surrounding area. This phenomenon explains Atlanta's strange meandering streets that curve and bend instead of sitting properly in a traditional grid like other American cities. In addition to its unique layout along rail lines, Atlanta's insatiable appetite for outward versus upward growth has made walking to many of the museums in the book impractical. However, you will soon find in the pages of this guide that there are clusters of museums that are easily accessible to each other.

Metropolitan Atlanta is best characterized as an indistinguishable connection of communities that are linked by a mutual past. Today Atlanta proper covers only 131 square miles and is home to 430,000 Georgians. The Atlanta metro area, however, sprawls across 1,963 square miles and is home to ten times that number of people. Two simultaneous forces have facilitated the growth of this megalopolis: the city's continued outward growth toward the small towns that have now become Atlanta suburbs (Kennesaw, Norcross, Marietta, Smyrna, Decatur, Jonesboro, and others) and the suburbs' continued growth toward the city. Once geographically separated from the city, they are now firmly woven into the fabric of Atlanta. As such, we have included the museums and historic homes found in these locations.

For the Civil War enthusiast, Atlanta has much to offer. William Tecumseh Sherman's famed March to the Sea began in northern Georgia in 1864 when he ordered 100,000 Union soldiers forward toward Atlanta and then on to the sea. By the time Sherman reached Savannah, the Union and Confederate Armies would fight 20 major battles in Georgia, many of them in and around Atlanta. After finally routing the Confederates during the Battle of Atlanta on July 22, 1864, Sherman's artillery set the city on fire and left it in ruins. For this, Atlanta owns a dubious distinction as the only major United States city to be completely destroyed by an invading army. Given the Civil War's impact on the city's psyche, visitors have many remarkable sites to tour, such as the Kennesaw Mountain National Battlefield, the Southern Museum of the Civil War & Locomotive History, and the Cyclorama. From Union-commandeered historic homes in Roswell to the storied adventure of a the "Great Locomotive Chase" that began in modern-day Kennesaw, Atlanta has a lifetime of tales to share about this epic American struggle. Thankfully, the city's important location as a transportation hub enabled it to make a complete recovery. Furthermore, Atlanta's first reinvention from antebellum stronghold to post–Civil War economic center gave the city a very un-Southern injection of new residents, as it was inundated with Yankee businessmen hoping to make their fortune in a resurgent Atlanta.

Throughout the Atlanta area are many historic homes open to the public, which provide a window into life in antebellum Georgia. Both the Atlanta History Center and Stone Mountain have amassed impressive collections of nineteenth-century outbuildings gathered from plantations and yeoman farms located throughout the state. These wooden structures have been painstakingly reassembled to give visitors a truly authentic rural Georgia experience. Other antebellum sites such as Bulloch Hall and The Archibald Smith Plantation Home in the northern Atlanta town of Roswell provide a glimpse into how many of Georgia's aristocracy lived in the mid-1800s. At one time this area was a popular summer retreat for the elite due to Atlanta's relatively mild summers compared to Savannah and the rest of the Georgia coast. Helping round out the story of Atlanta's early families, the Herndon Home epitomizes the city's unique African American experience. The house is located on the west side of town. Built in 1910 by Alonzo Herndon, a former slave turned insurance and real estate mogul, the Herndon Home serves as a poignant reminder of one man's determination to overcome the burdens of his past, memorializing the success of many black business people throughout the difficult segregation era of Atlanta.

Fittingly, Atlanta is the city of Martin Luther King, Jr., who devoted his life to dismantling the codified prejudice of the Old South. In addition to touring his birth home, visitors to The Martin Luther King, Jr., National Historic Site and King Center can sit in the Ebeneezer Baptist Church to hear recordings of MLK's most famous sermons and speeches. The city blocks surrounding these important sites are bustling with new life as more and more people are choosing to live in the city. Over the last five years, Atlanta has enjoyed a robust urban renewal that continues to spread across all sections of the city. With the influx of people has come an explosion of new restaurants and coffee shops and calls for more green space.

A second world leader and fellow Nobel Prize winner who calls Atlanta home is Jimmy Carter. The Carter Center and Jimmy Carter presidential library and museum preserve the legacy of a man who started as a peanut farmer in Plains, Georgia; served as the 39th President of the United States; and then captured international acclaim as a champion of waging peace, fighting disease, and building hope. Here in Atlanta, the Carter Center and presidential library enrich the city through educational and outreach programs.

Atlanta has also given us Margaret Mitchell, who wrote nostalgically of the Old South in *Gone with the Wind*. More than any other southern writer, Mitchell painted a vividly romantic picture of the Old South that has enchanted countless millions around the world. Margaret Mitchell's legacy has left an indelible mark on Atlanta as reflected by the many museums across the city dedicated to her monumental novel. After being adapted to the big screen, where it was phenomenally successful, *Gone with the Wind* is now widely considered to be the most popular and enduring film of all time. Three must-see stops that tell the story of Tara and its creator are the Marietta Gone With the Wind Museum: Scarlett on the Square in Marietta, the famed Margaret Mitchell House and Museum in Midtown, and the Road to Tara Museum in Jonesboro. For the most devoted Margaret Mitchell fan, you can visit Oakland Cemetery, which is located in the heart of Atlanta, to pay your respects at her gravesite.

Another notable Atlantan buried in Oakland Cemetery is golfer Bobby Jones. Jones symbolizes the competitive spirit of the city and is Atlanta's first true sports hero. The Atlanta History Center has an entire permanent exhibit showcasing his athletic prowess. Between 1923 and 1930, Jones was unstoppable, winning 13 out of the 21 major tournaments in which he played. In 1930 he accomplished the impossible by winning the U.S. Open, British Open, and U.S. Amateur Championship all in the same year—a feat that has never been duplicated.

Sports fans of all ages can cheer on a variety of college and professional teams that call the city home. From the Georgia Tech Yellow Jackets, where John Heisman (of football's Heisman Trophy fame) coached the school to its first national championship in 1917 to the Atlanta Braves, which have essentially become America's team by winning 14 consecutive division titles, the thrill of watching competitive teams has always had a strong grip on the people of Atlanta. Baseball fans can take a tour of Turner Field, which begins in the Ivan Allen, Jr., Atlanta Braves Museum and Hall of Fame. From the upper deck of Turner Field, visitors on the tour can look down into the old Fulton County stadium where Hammerin' Hank Aaron hit his 715th career home run and broke Babe Ruth's all-time home run record on April 8, 1974.

In addition to the sports prowess of its Georgia Tech Yellow Jackets, the university is recognized as a world-renowned academic center. Visitors to Atlanta can stop and tour its Robert C. Williams Paper Museum, a global resource on the history of papermaking. After learning about thousands of years of papermaking, you can head across the city to Emory University's Michael C. Carlos Museum, which boasts the

Southeast's largest collection of antiquities and ancient art from Egypt, Greece, Rome, the Near East, and Pre-Columbian America. Two other notable college museums are the Spelman College Museum of Fine Art and the Clark Atlanta University Collections of African American Art. The Spelman and Clark galleries are within walking distance of each other and contain world-class artwork.

The city's mother lode of artwork, a collection of over 11,000 pieces, is found in the High Museum, which is located in Midtown. The High's recent and impressive 177,000 square-foot expansion exemplifies the communities' devotion to supporting the arts. However, the dozens of smaller galleries, museums, and artist cooperatives across the city provide the base for young artists to thrive and for the residents to enjoy their uninhibited art. There is quite a range of contemporary, folk, and fine art to enjoy in locations like the Contemporary, the Apex Museum, and the Hammonds House Galleries. A fun and nontraditional museum not to miss is located in the Center for Puppetry Arts, which celebrates the history of this amazing art form. This book focuses on those galleries in the city that are largely noncommercial in nature, although it should be noted that there are many wonderful galleries outside of these confines.

The city has also enjoyed a long love affair with the corporations that have made the city famous. Of these, Coca-Cola is the oldest and most renowned worldwide. The World of Coca-Cola museum explains the company's meteoric rise to fame from humble beginnings in 1886 to its current status as a global marketing machine. Ted Turner also left an unmistakable mark on the city when he created CNN, the world's first live

24-hour news television network, followed by other such stations as TBS, TNT, and the Cartoon Network. A tour of the CNN studios is certainly a must-see for all. For the aviation enthusiasts, the Delta Air Transport Heritage Museum maintains vintage aircraft on site, as this international airline is also headquartered in Atlanta.

Ironically, there is no end in sight for the city once called Terminus. Modern-day Atlanta owes its existence to being at the right place at the right time. Originally a small town sitting at the junction of railroads, Atlanta continues to command national and international attention. As the once all-too-important railways have given way to a vibrant crisscrossing of interstates, Atlanta continues to draw unique personalities, businesses, and ideas into its thriving community.

We hope this museum guide motivates and provides you with the necessary information to explore this great city. Support and awareness is what keeps Atlanta's history and museums alive. Unfortunately, institutions like the Atlanta Museum of the late antique collector James H. Elliott, Jr., have already closed their doors. To ensure that Atlanta's history stays here for all to enjoy, we encourage you to visit these institutions and support their fund-raising efforts.

Using *Museums of Atlanta*

The 68 museums in this guide are listed in alphabetical order by the primary name of the museum or collection. Each entry provides the address, phone number, and Web site for the museum as well as when it is open and what the admission fees are. Since that information can change, it's important to confirm before you go, especially with smaller museums dependent on volunteer help. Calling ahead will inform you about special events and programs, temporary exhibits, and any exhibition that may require additional ticketing. Many museums do not charge an admission fee, but donations are always welcome even when one is not suggested.

Each entry also features symbols to provide a quick reference to tell you if the museum has exhibits for children, if it's best to provide your own transportation, or if you must call ahead before visiting. A key to all of theses symbols is at the end of this section.

Museums are indicated on the maps by page number, making it easy to find which museums are near each other. Some are in or within walking distance of the downtown business district or are easily accessed by bus or train. Other museums that dot the city and suburbs do require a car. Calling a museum or consulting with an MARTA agent will help you find public transportation or the best driving route to your destination.

Following the last museum entry is a section listing museums by different categories, such as the best museums to see on a short trip, those most enjoyable for young children, and the major museums for art, history, or science. These are designed to give guidance in planning your visit.

Further Reading and Resources

Allen, Frederick. *Atlanta Rising: The Invention of an International City 1946–1996*. Athens, Ga.: Longstreet Press, 1996.

Buffington, Perry and Kim Underwood. *Archival Atlanta Forgotten Facts and Well Kept Secrets From Our City's Past*. Atlanta: Peachtree Publishers, 1996.

Craig, Richard M. *Atlanta Architecture: Art Deco to Modern Classic, 1929–1959*. Gretna, La.: Pelican, 1995.

Pomerantz, Gary M. *Where Peachtree Meets Sweet Auburn: A Saga of Race and Family*. New York: Penguin, 1996.

Visitor Information

Atlanta Convention & Visitors Bureau

233 Peachtree Street, NE

Suite 100

Atlanta, GA 30303

404-521-6600

info@atlanta.net

www.atlanta.net

Open: M–F, 9:00 AM–5:00 PM

The mission of the Atlanta Convention & Visitors Bureau (AVCB) is to provide Atlanta's 19 million annual visitors with information about the city's vibrant economy as well as its cultural attractions. Established in 1913, the AVCB functions as Atlanta's liaison with meeting planners, tour operators, and individual tourists, who generate $3.5 billion a year for Atlanta. The organization's Web site is an excellent starting point for anyone planning a business or personal trip to the city of Atlanta.

Atlanta Preservation Center
327 St. Paul Avenue
Atlanta, GA 30312
404-688-3353
Tour hotline: 404-688-3350
www.preserveatlanta.com

The Atlanta Preservation Center's 80 trained volunteers lead almost 10,000 people a year on guided tours of Atlanta's six historic districts. The center's main focus, however, is to work with business, government, and community leaders to preserve Atlanta's historic buildings. Since its founding in 1980, the center has ensured the preservation of over 140 commercial and residential buildings.

Regional Transportation

Atlanta's sprawling growth has made transportation a challenge for visitors and residents. Known as "the lowest-density large urbanized area in the world," Atlanta's four million residents are spread out across 1,963 square miles. Serving much of the area is MARTA, Atlanta's public-transportaion system. However, reaching a final destinaion often requires changing from the subway to a bus. Since few of the desitinations described in the guide are within walking distance of each other, plan accordingly if traveling via public transportation.

MARTA (Metropolitan Atlanta Regional Transportation Authority)
2424 Piedmont Road, NE
Atlanta, GA 30324-3311
404-848-5000
schedinfo@itsmarta.com
www.itsmarta.com

Downloadable and configurable maps are available at MARTA's Web site, which provides the most current information about bus and rail schedules. Agents are available by phone from 7:00 AM to 6:00 PM Monday through Friday. Recorded information is available from 6:00 AM to 11:00 PM Monday through Friday and 8:00 AM to 10:00 PM Saturday, Sunday, and holidays.

Maps

Each museum in this book is marked on the following maps by its page number. These maps are designed to show the reader the general proximity of the museums to one another.

Museums of Atlanta

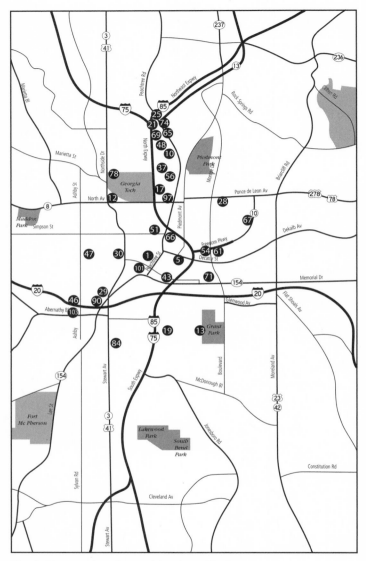

Map 1. Museums in and around downtown Atlanta.
(Each number is a museum's book page.)

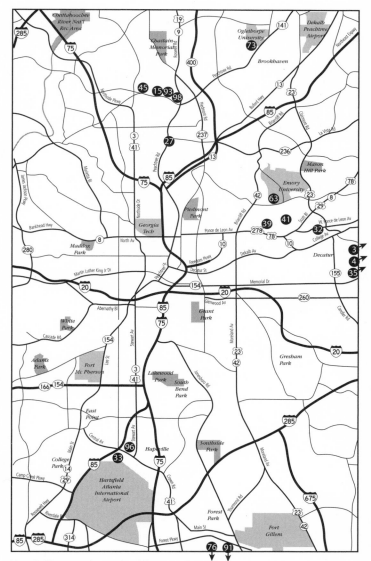

Map 2. Museums in greater Atlanta.

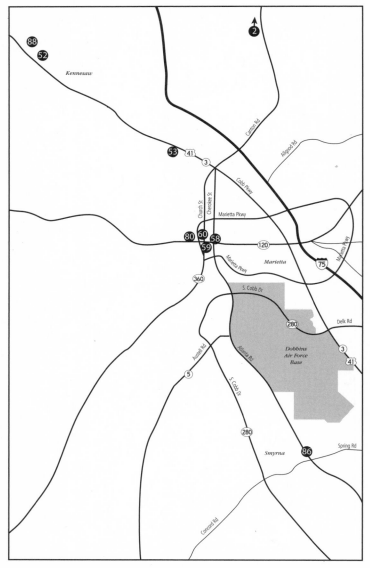

Map 3. Museums northwest of Atlanta (Marietta and Kennesaw).

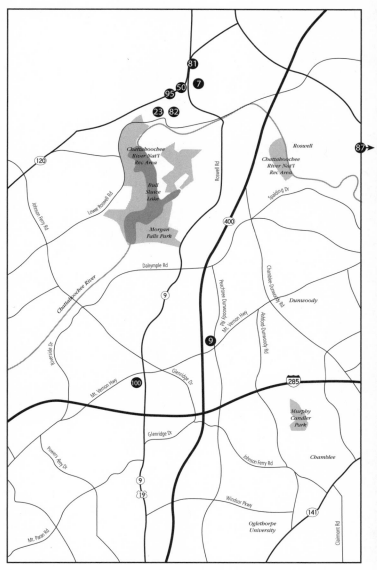

Map 4. Museums northeast of Atlanta (Roswell).

Visual Codes

Architecturally significant

Exhibits suitable for children

Best to provide own transportation

Food available on premises

Must call ahead

Notable art

Notable grounds or garden

Science oriented

Site of historic event

The Africa World Museum and Center

134 Peachtree Street (Map 1)
404-588-0404
Open: M–Sa, 10:00 AM–7:00 PM
Admission: Free

Drawn from over 500 leading African artists from 54 African countries, the revolving exhibits shown at the Africa World Museum and Center are designed to educate visitors about Africa's past, present, and future. The museum itself is a combination gallery, workshop, education center, and gift shop. The two floors of the gallery showcase both traditional and contemporary African art in a variety of media: wood carvings, cow horns, wood burnings, metal plates, collages, and batiks. In addition to celebrating each Independence Day of Africa's 54 nations, the Africa World Museum and Center organizes events and educational programs on African music, food, clothing, language, and jewelry. Documentaries on African life and culture are also shown throughout the year.

Air Acres

376 Air Acres Way (Map 3)
Woodstock
770-517-6090 or 770-569-4613
http://airacresmuseum.home.mindspring.com
Open: No set schedule. Call ahead for hours.
Admission: Free

The Air Acres Museum is much more of an active celebration of the past than the traditional museum. Located in a small hangar on a private runway, this facility is committed to maintaining and rebuilding past military and private aircraft. Owned and funded by a private entrepreneur, Air Acres has a changing rotation of planes on display, depending on what is currently being restored. These planes are kept in flying condition and can often be found moving in and out of the hangar during a visit. Stop by and discuss the planes' histories with these knowledgeable craftspeople.

Antebellum Plantation at Stone Mountain

John B. Gordon Drive (Map 2)
Stone Mountain Park
770-413-5229
www.stonemountainpark.com
Open: M–Th, 10:00 AM–5:00 PM; F & Su, 10:00 AM–6:00 PM; Sa, 10:00 AM–7:00 PM
Admission: $7.00; Children under 3, free. To enter Stone Mountain Park, visitors must purchase one $8.00 permit per vehicle.

The Antebellum Plantation at Stone Mountain provides visitors with a unique opportunity to tour 15 original plantation buildings built between 1790 and 1845 at different locations throughout Georgia. Each of the structures represents the best of eighteenth- and nineteenth-century craftsmanship. Reassembled in one location in the Stone Mountain Park, the buildings are configured to give visitors an authentic look at antebellum Georgia. Well-constructed walkways enable guests to move freely among the buildings. Stone Mountain Park has created a highly informative self-tour pamphlet that gives the purpose and history of each of the reconstructed buildings.

Highlights:
Thornton House, which was built circa 1790 and is one of the oldest restored homes in Georgia
Animals housed in the farmyard next to the Dickey House
Civil War reenactors drilling on the plantation grounds (Check the Web site for dates and times.)

The Antique Car and Treasure Museum

Robert E. Lee Boulevard (Map 2)
Stone Mountain Park
770-413-5229
www.stonemountainpark.com
Open: W–Su, noon–6:00 PM; Sa, noon–7:00 PM
Admission: Adults, $7.00; Children, $4.00. To enter Stone Mountain
Park, visitors must purchase one $8.00 permit per vehicle.

Named one of the top ten small car museums in the United
States by *Car Collector* magazine, the Antique Car and
Treasure Museum at Stone Mountain is filled with all things
Americana. The museum showcases 50 years of collectables
amassed by the Protsman family of Georgia. On display with
the automobiles are jukeboxes, player pianos, carousel animals,
barber poles, antique toys, beaded purses, and electric trains.
Also featured prominently in the museum are over 70 antique
bicycles, which are in pristine condition. Their incredibly
graceful frames and vibrant colors highlight the craftsmanship
of manufacturers such as Shelby, Huffman, and Dayton during
the 1940s and 1950s. Many of the museum's vehicles are the
only ones known to exist in the world. Among the automobiles
in the museum is the famous 1948 Tucker, which was featured
in the Hollywood movie *Tucker: The Man and his Dream*. Only
51 of these cars were manufactured.

Highlights:

Rare motorized vehicles such as a 1904 one-cylinder, seven-
horsepower Oldsmobile pie wagon

Antique bicycles made by the Indian Motorcycle Company

A 1930 Rolls Royce Town Car

The APEX Museum

135 Auburn Avenue (Map 1)
404-521-APEX (2739)
www.apexmuseum.org
Open: Tu–Sa, 10:00 AM–5:00 PM; Su, 1:00 PM–5:00 PM (Su hours
only during the months of February, June, July, and August)
Admission: Adults, $4.00; Seniors and Students, $3.00; Children under
4 and Members, free

In April 1900, W. E. B. DuBois traveled to Paris, France, to
oversee an exhibit entitled "The Georgia Negro" at the
World's Fair in the French capital. The exhibit was the brain-
child of Thomas J. Calloway, an African American lawyer and
educator, who wanted to show the world that African
Americans were an economic force to be appreciated and
respected. To get the project off the ground, Calloway enlisted
the help of DuBois and Booker T. Washington, who were
able to convince then-president William McKinley to support
the project. Today the APEX Museum houses a recreation of
the exhibit along with a replica of the Moses Amos drug store.
Moses Amos was the founder of the first African
American–owned drug store in Atlanta. In addition to these
two displays, visitors can see prominent African Americans
featured in the Hall of Achievement as well as watch a ten-
minute film called *The Journey* narrated by Ossie Davis.

Highlights:
Georgia Black Codes from the 1800s posted in the museum
(including one that stipulates anyone caught buying certain
commodities from slaves would get 39 lashes)

A wall of photographs showing scenes from everyday life of African Americans in the 1800s and early 1900s

Economic data contained in "The Georgia Negro" exhibit

Archibald Smith Plantation Home

935 Alpharetta Street (Map 4)

Roswell

770-641-3978

www.archibaldsmithplantation.org

Open: M–F, 11:30 AM–2:30 PM (tours on the half hour); Sa, 10:30 AM–1:30 PM (tours on the half hour)

Admission: Adults, $8.00; Children 6–12, $6.00; Children 6 and under, free

Built with slave labor in 1845 on land made available by the forcible removal of Cherokee Indians, the Archibald Smith Plantation Home provides a fascinating window into the complexity of the Old South. Adding to the uniqueness of the plantation is the fact that the only inhabitants of the home were three generations of Archibald Smith's family and one African American cook, Mamie Cotton, who outlived all of the Smiths and lived in the house by herself until her death in 1994. Luckily for historians and today's visitors, the three generations of Smiths that lived in the house were pack rats, saving everything from clothing and old letters to farm tools and antique toys. When the last surviving member of the Smith family died in 1981, a group of nephews and nieces cataloged the more than 14,000 items that had been tucked into every nook and cranny in the house as well as its outbuildings. Today visitors can tour the Archibald Smith Plantation and its 12 original outbuildings, which include slave cabins and a stone spring house. Throughout the year, the barn houses various exhibits drawn from the 14,000 Smith family artifacts.

Highlights:

A detailed exhibit of photographs showing formal and candid images of all three generations of the Smith family and Mamie Cotton

The story of Willie Smith's fateful decision to return home via North Carolina to avoid Sherman's March: how he evaded one danger only to succumb to another

The Art Institute of Atlanta: Janet S. Day Gallery

6600 Peachtree Dunwoody Road (Map 4)

100 Embassy Row, NE

770-394-8300

www.aia.artinstitutes.edu/gallery.asp

Open: M–Th, 9:00 AM–8:00 PM; F, 9:00 AM–4:00 PM; Sa, 9:00 AM–3:00 PM

Admission: Free

The Janet S. Day Gallery is located on the first floor of the Art Institute building. It is a small but beautiful space adjacent to the front office of the school. This gallery is perfect to enjoy over a lunch or when looking for a break in the day. The gallery features student, faculty, and graduate work as well as traveling exhibits. The Art Institute states that its goals for the space are to inspire and challenge students through examples of accomplished artists, to enrich the learning community at the Art Institute of Atlanta through exhibitions that demonstrate high levels of excellence, to provide opportunities to increase public awareness of the Art Institute of Atlanta and its importance in the art community, and to expose the local community to relevant faculty, student, and professional work.

Atlanta College of Art: ACA Gallery & Gallery 100

1280 Peachtree Street, NE (Map 1)
404-733-5050
www.aca.edu/gall_main.htm
Admission: Free

Located on the first floor of the Woodruff Arts Center on Peachtree Street, the ACA Gallery and Gallery 100 are located in the heart of Midtown in Atlanta's art center. We encourage checking the Web site for the latest exhibition schedule and hours, since both galleries' operations are connected to the Atlanta College of Art's academic schedule.

ACA Gallery

Open: Tu–Th, 11:00 AM–5:00 PM; F, 11:00 AM–8:00 PM; Sa & Su, noon–5:00 PM (summer); Tu, W, Sa, 10:00 AM–5:00 PM; Th & F, 10:00 AM–9:30 PM; Su, noon–5:00 PM (academic year)

Focused on exploring contemporary art, the ACA Gallery displays not only work of ACA students and faculty but also sources from nationally and internationally known artists. The gallery has gained recognition since its 1996 renovation and was recently named best gallery in Atlanta by *Creative Loafing* newspaper. The gallery hosts eight to ten exhibits annually that display a variety of styles and media within contemporary art.

Gallery 100

Open: M–Su, 9:00 AM–9:00 PM

Gallery 100 is committed to showcasing the rising talents of the students at the Atlanta College of Art. All media are explored in this space and exhibits change weekly. The gallery contains a wide range of styles as it showcases students' efforts to master expressions of the past as well as explore and develop new artistic territory.

Atlanta Contemporary Art Center (the Contemporary)

535 Means Street, NW (Map 1)
404-688-1970
www.thecontemporary.org
Open: Tu–Sa, 11:00 AM–5:00 PM
Admission: Adults, $5.00; Seniors, Students, and Children, $3.00

Originally founded in 1973 as the Nexus Contemporary Art Center, the Contemporary has become a focal point for the Atlanta art community. The center was originally created as an artist-run cooperative but has since evolved into a multidisciplinary contemporary art museum that exposes Atlanta to local, national, and international artists. The center showcases five unique exhibitions a year, augmented with other presentations as well. The exhibits focus on current ideas within contemporary artistic expression from both individuals and groups of artists. While the artwork on display is the focal point, the Contemporary is also quite involved in local art education and takes an active role in fostering a cooperative artist community. Twelve studio spaces are on location, which have been awarded to emerging, mid-career, and established professional artists as a subsidized means to explore new ideas, collaboration, and exploration. Call ahead or check the Web site for the most current exhibit information.

Atlanta Cyclorama and Civil War Museum

800 Cherokee Avenue, SE (Map 1)

404-624-1071

Open: M–Su, 8:50 AM–4:30 PM

Admission: Adults, $7.00; Seniors, $6.00; Children 6–12, $5.00; Children under 6, free

In the nineteenth century, before motion pictures were invented, average citizens attended viewings of gigantic circular paintings known as cycloramas. At the height of their popularity, over 300 different cycloramas were shown throughout the world. Today there are only 20 in existence—three of which are located in the United States. At four stories tall, 458 feet in circumference, and weighing 9,000 pounds, the Atlanta Cyclorama, which depicts the Battle of Atlanta, is truly a remarkable oil painting. In 1886 the American Panorama Company recruited 11 German artists for this project who had worked on panoramic paintings of the Franco-Prussian War. At that time, it took over two years to complete and cost $42,000. A recent appraisal of the giant canvas valued the painting at $14,000,000. In addition to viewing the cyclorama, visitors can see the locomotive *Texas*, which was used by Confederate forces to run down and recapture one of its locomotives, the *General*, stolen by Union forces. There are also wonderful exhibits of Civil War artifacts, including muskets and pistols, as well as actual playing cards and dominoes used by soldiers in camp.

For *Gone With the Wind enthusiasts*, we recommend purchasing the Premiere Pass, which includes five separate attractions: Atlanta Cyclorama and Civil War Museum, Historical & Hysterical Tours (costumed guided car tour to various locations in Jonesboro, GA), Margaret Mitchell House, Road to Tara Museum, and Stately Oaks Plantation.

Highlights:

A James Earl Jones–narrated short film on the campaign leading up to the Battle of Atlanta

A narrated viewing of the cyclorama that highlights its details and ironies

A Confederate soldier's wooden canteen with corncob plug

The Atlanta History Center

130 West Paces Ferry Road, NW (Map 2)
404-814-4000
www.atlhist.org
Open: M–Sa, 10:00 AM–5:30 PM; Su, noon–5:30 PM
Admission: Adults, $15.00; Seniors and Students 13 & up, $12.00;
Children 4–12, $10.00, Children under 3 and Members, free

One of the largest history museums in the southeast, the
Atlanta History Center is unquestionably the keeper of
Atlanta's, and the South's, rich and storied past. In addition to
its main exhibition space, the Atlanta History Center's 33-acre
campus contains the Tullie Smith Farm, the Swan House, and
a research library and archives used by 10,000 people annually.
Housed in the Atlanta History Center's main exhibition space
are four signature exhibitions that were funded through two
multimillion-dollar capital campaigns during the 1990s. Upon
entering the center, visitors should first walk through
Metropolitan Frontiers: Atlanta 1835–2000, the center's first
and oldest signature exhibition. Created to celebrate the rise
and evolution of one of America's great cities, the exhibition
reminds visitors that Atlanta has had a tumultuous history in
which events have tested, but never broken, the resolve of the
city's remarkable citizens. An amazing gift anchors Turning
Point: The American Civil War, the center's next signature
exhibition. In 1986 the DuBose family presented the Atlanta
History Center with 5,000 Civil War artifacts collected by
Beverly M. DuBose, Jr., and his son, Beverly M. DuBose III
over a 40-year period. The DuBose collection is one of the
most important private Civil War collections ever assembled.

The curators of the exhibition have done an outstanding job in the creative layout of the artifacts so that moving through the space allows visitors to experience the vastness and complexity of this defining period in American history. The museum's final two signature exhibitions are Shaping Traditions: Folk Arts in a Changing South and Down the Fairway with Bobby Jones. For hundreds of years, Southern folk artists, both white and black, have created fascinating pottery and textiles as well as mesmerizing music. Folk Arts in a Changing South takes visitors on a journey through all of these media. Down the Fairway with Bobby Jones does an excellent job showcasing the highlights of Jones's career. The exhibition also shows the evolution of the game's clubs and equipment while dedicating space to pioneering women and African American golfers that history has forgotten. In addition to its four signature exhibitions, the Atlanta History Center also has two galleries that house changing exhibitions. Strolling through its exhibition space as well as its surrounding 33-acre campus, visitors can readily see that the Atlanta History Center does indeed accomplish its mission of "connecting people to the past so they may better understand the present and prepare for the future."

Atlanta's Fox Theatre

660 Peachtree Street, NE (Map 1)
404-688-3353
www.foxtheatre.org
Open: Tours M, W, F, 10:00 AM
Admission: Adults, $10.00; Seniors and Students, $5.00

Built originally as Yaarab Temple Shrine Mosque, the Shriner's national headquarters in the late 1920s, the Fox Theatre's opulent interior and funky exterior have enchanted Atlanta for over 80 years. In addition to showing countless films, the theater has become Atlanta's destination for Broadway plays and has featured performers ranging from the Metropolitan Opera to the Rolling Stones. Today the Fox is listed on the National Register of Historic Places, which is remarkable given the theater's many brushes with bankruptcy and threats of demolition. The most serious threat occurred in the mid-1970s when the theater was nearly sold to SouthernBell, which had plans to tear down the theater to make room for a new headquarters building. Refusing to accept this outcome, a group of civic-minded Atlantans launched a four-year Save the Fox campaign that saved the theater and put it back on solid financial footing. Touring the Fox enables visitors to experience what one journalist described as "a picturesque and almost disturbing grandeur beyond imagination." The tour guides are knowledgeable and bring this fascinating building to life.

Highlights:
Mighty Mo, the Fox's massive pipe organ, which has 3,622 different pipes

The indoor Arabian Courtyard complete with drifting clouds and a twinkling sky

The Braves Museum and Hall of Fame

755 Hank Aaron Drive, SW (Map 1)

404-614-2311

www.bravesmuseum.com

Open: M–F, 9:00 AM–3:00 PM; Sa & Su, 1:00 PM–3:00 PM
(Apr.–Sept.); Call ahead or check the Web site for game day schedule;
M–Sa, 10:00 AM–2:00 PM (Oct.–Mar.)

Admission: Stadium tour—Adults, $10.00; Children, $5.00; Groups of
20 or more, $7.00. Museum—during games, $2.00; nongame days,
$5.00

With 14 straight division titles and a rich and storied history,
the Atlanta Braves are one of the most heralded sports fran-
chises in the United States. For the people of Atlanta, the
Braves sit at the confluence of major forces that built and con-
tinue to shape the city. Atlanta icon Ted Turner developed
Turner Field, the present home of the Atlanta Braves, to serve
as the venue for the opening and closing ceremonies of the 1996
Summer Olympics. After the Olympics, it was modified into
its present configuration as a baseball stadium. Hank Aaron
made history next to Turner Field in the old Fulton County
stadium, where he hit his 715th home run, pushing him past
Babe Ruth. And no visit to the Ted, the nickname given to the
stadium by Atlanta natives, is complete without a Coca-Cola,
another local institution, which advertises heavily throughout
Turner Field. A tour of the Braves Hall of Fame quickly
reminds visitors that the team has also called Boston and
Milwaukee home. The Braves enjoy a unique history that
began in Boston in 1871, making the Braves the oldest continually running franchise in the major leagues. On display in the

Hall of Fame is memorabilia from Brave greats such as Hank Aaron and Phil Neikro. It is a must-see for even the casual fan. After enjoying the Hall of Fame, visitors can take an hour-long guided tour of Turner Field. Stops include Coca-Cola Sky Field, a luxury suite, the press box, the broadcast booth, the locker room, and the Braves dugout.

Highlights:

Warren Spahn's United States Army uniform and Purple Heart Medal awarded for wounds received during the Second World War

Knowledgeable tour guides who explain the interconnectedness of the Braves with the city of Atlanta

Exhibits on the Atlanta Crackers and Atlanta Black Crackers, the city's white and black baseball teams that predated the arrival of the Braves

The Breman: The William Breman Jewish Heritage Museum

1440 Spring Street (at 18th Street; Map 1)

678-222-3700

www.thebreman.org

Open: M–Th, 10:00 AM–5:00 PM; F, 10:00 AM–3:00 PM; Su, 1:00 PM–5:00 PM. Closed most Jewish and secular holidays.

Admission: Adults, $10.00; Seniors, $6.00; Students, $4.00; Children 3–6, $2.00; Members and Children under 3, free

The Breman maintains two core galleries ("Creating Community: The Jews of Atlanta from 1845 to Present" and "Absence of Humanity: The Holocaust Years"), a special-exhibits gallery (hosting three to four exhibits annually), archives, a center for Holocaust education, a library, and a children's discovery center. The Creating Community exhibit tells the story of Atlanta Jewish history, from the first immigrants to present day. For those unfamiliar with Jewish customs, this is an excellent introduction to Jewish family life and the rituals that bind the Jewish people. The growth of the Jewish community within Atlanta is also chronicled and features two engaging local tragedies, the Leo Frank trial and the Temple bombing. The Absence of Humanity exhibit features insight into the rise of Nazi Germany and the deliberate deterioration of Jewish liberties, finally resulting in the horrors of the Holocaust. Designed by local survivor, Ben Hirsch, the exhibit explains this tragedy by highlighting the effects on individual lives using extensive personal memorabilia, family letters, photographs, and testimonials. This incredibly moving piece is a must-see. The special exhibit gallery features local, national, and international exhibits that portray Jewish culture and heritage. Check the Web site or call for current features.

Highlights:

Legacy Project—an interactive Internet project with streaming video, photographs, and interviews of local Atlanta Holocaust survivors telling their individual stories

Videos of the highly publicized Leo Frank trial and the Temple bombing

Bulloch Hall

180 Bulloch Avenue (Map 4)
Roswell
770-992-1731
www.bullochhall.org
Open: M–Sa, 10:00 AM–3:00 PM; Su, 1:00 PM–3:00 PM. Tours on the hour.
Admission: Adults $8.00; Children 6–12, $6.00

Built in 1840 by Major James Stephen Bulloch, the stately Greek Revival mansion known as Bulloch Hall boasts a fascinating connection to two United States presidents. On December 22, 1853, Major Bulloch's daughter Mittie married Theodore Roosevelt, Sr., in Bulloch Hall. Their son, Theodore Roosevelt, Jr., became the 26th president of the United States in 1901. Mittie also produced a famous granddaughter, Eleanor Roosevelt, who married Franklin Delano Roosevelt, the 32nd president of the United States. Consequently, the former Mittie Bulloch of Bulloch Hall has the distinction of being the only person to have a son serve as a United States president and a granddaughter serve as a First Lady. The tour of Bulloch Hall takes visitors through the classic four-square plantation home, with an impressive center hallway and two rooms off each side. Visitors can also see the family's bedrooms upstairs as well as an exhibit on the Roosevelt and Bulloch families. The basement of the home contains the kitchen with its beehive oven and sunken root cellar. On the grounds of Bulloch Hall are reconstructed slave quarters as well as 142 trees on the Historic Tree Register. Today Bulloch Hall hosts a variety of community events and is home to local guilds that preserve the skills and craftsmanship of the nine-teenth century.

Highlights:

Photographs of President Theodore Roosevelt's visit to Bulloch Hall in 1905

The meticulously manicured grounds, which give a truly authentic feel to the Bulloch Hall experience

Center for Puppetry Arts

1404 Spring Street, NW (at 18th Street; Map 1)

404-873-3391

www.puppet.org

Open: Tu–Sa, 9:00 AM–5:00 PM; Su, 11:00 AM–5:00 PM

Admission: Adults, $8.00; Seniors and Students, $7.00; Children, $6.00; Members and those with full-priced show admission, free. Behind-the-scenes tour: with single-show purchase, $5.00; Members, $4.00

While relatively obscure in American culture, puppetry has long been a discrete and popular art form in many international communities. The Center for Puppetry Arts explores the history, varied cultural interpretations, and social impacts of puppetry. Housing over 1,000 puppets and scores of books and videotapes, this museum is wonderfully interactive, educational, and fun for children as well as adults. Its intent is to introduce this international art form to the American public as an instrument for teaching lessons and documenting everyday life of local communities. The museum's permanent collection, Puppets: The Power of Wonder, showcases over 350 puppets from all over the world and from different time periods. The exhibit explains a variety of common dramatic stage techniques such as lighting and color and offers them in interactive manner for children to explore. The collection also includes many handmade puppets from Thailand, Africa, and Europe and explains the different theatrical methods used in those areas. Be sure to check the current listings to enjoy one of the puppet shows while visiting the museum.

Highlights:

Puppet Arcade—hand puppet theaters and mechanically controlled puppets

Actual body puppet of Skesis, one of the characters from the famous Jim Henson movie *The Dark Crystal*

Behind-the-scenes tour with the puppeteers before show

Video of Wayland Flowers' *Madame*, the often raunchy but famous Las Vegas and New York City act

The Chastain Gallery

135 West Wieuca Road, NW (Map 2)
404-252-2927
Open: M–Sa, 1:00 PM–5:00 PM
Admission: Free

Known for its innovative exhibitions, the Chastain Gallery enjoys an international reputation for its pioneering contemporary art shows. Through the years, visitors have enjoyed everything from black-and-white photography to oil paintings to other unique visual media. The published mission of the Chastain Gallery is "to expose the Atlanta community to exhibitions that address the social and political issues of our time." Nestled in the low wooded hills in Buckhead, the gallery is housed in a series of buildings that includes the Chastain Arts Center, one of Atlanta's oldest community art centers. The gallery space is airy and friendly. Enjoy it after a late lunch or during a trip to Chastain Park. Call ahead for specifics on current exhibits.

City Gallery East

675 Ponce De Leon Avenue, NE (Map 1)
404-817-6999
www.bcaatlanta.com/index.php?pid=88
Open: M–Sa, 10:00 AM–5:00 PM
Admission: Free

Complete with hardwood floors and exposed, loft-style ceilings, City Gallery East comprises 8,000 square feet in the City Hall East building, which is located on Ponce de Leon Avenue. Before being occupied by the city government, the two million square feet of the City Hall East building gained notoriety as the backdrop for thousands of game-day photos for both the Atlanta Crackers and the Atlanta Black Crackers, the two professional baseball teams that played in Atlanta before the arrival of the Atlanta Braves. One of Atlanta's largest exhibition spaces, the City Gallery East has been a mainstay in the efforts of the Atlanta Bureau of Cultural Affairs to promote local artists since 1993. Adding to its allure is the gallery's dual purpose: it also functions as a massive walkway through the lower part of the City Hall East building. City workers, art enthusiasts, and policemen cross paths in the space, giving visitors an immediate sense that the exhibits are by the people and for the people. The gallery is able to strip away the aloofness accompanying many contemporary art experiences. This large exhibition area, well off the beaten path, makes a great side trip.

Clark Atlanta University Collections of African American Art

223 James P. Brawley Drive, SW (Map 1)
404-880-6644
Open: M–F, 10:00 AM–4:00 PM
Admission: Suggested donation, $3.00

Located on the second floor of the Trevor Arnett Hall on the Morehouse College campus, the Clark Atlanta University Collections of African American Art has a wonderful and fascinating history. From 1942 to 1970, Trevor Arnett Hall hosted the Atlanta Annuals, the nation's premier venue for African Americans to display their artwork. During most of this 29-year period, segregation prevented African Americans from showing their art in cultural institutions across the United States. However, at Trevor Arnett Hall more than 900 black artists from across the nation competed in the Atlanta Annuals. Taking center stage was the creative genius of artists such as Jacob Lawrence, Robert Blackburn, Elizabeth Catlett, William H. Johnson, Lois Mailou Jones, and Charles White. Today the Clark Atlanta University Collections of African American Art boasts more than 950 objects in a collection with four distinct sections: African American Art, African Art, Contemporary Art, and Art of the Negro Murals. In addition to exhibiting pieces of its permanent collection, the museum features artwork from various artists around the country as part of its mission to "cultivate a representative collection of American art and to encourage scholarly research, with special attention to the development of African American artists in the historical context of American art."

CNN Studio Tour

One CNN Center (Map 1)
404-827-2300
www.cnn.com/StudioTour
Open: M–Su, 9:00 AM–5:00 PM; Tours every ten minutes
Admission: Adults, $12.00; Seniors, $11.00; Children 4–18, $9.00;
Children under 4, free

Established in 1980 by Ted Turner, the Cable News Network (CNN) was the world's first 24-hour cable television news channel. CNN has changed the way the people of the world receive breaking news stories. To tour its facilities on the studio tour is to literally witness history being broadcast into living rooms, coffee shops, and government offices around the world. The tour begins with a ride up an eight-story escalator, one of the largest in the world, and ends in the control room theater where a tour guide explains exactly how the production of the news is managed. This explanation occurs while live footage of actual CNN producers overseeing the creation of the news is fed into the room. The next stop is a mock studio where the tour guide shares teleprompter secrets and demystifies the special effects used during different parts of the news broadcast. The tour continues past the studios of the different CNN channels that make up CNN News Group networks, which are broadcast to domestic as well as international audiences in a variety of languages. The final stop on the tour is a filmed testimonial of CNN broadcasters such as Christiane Amanpour and Wolf Blitzer sharing very personal thoughts on what it means to share the news with the world.

Highlights:

Watching actual news programming being created in real time

The professionalism and knowledge of the tour guides

Dekalb History Museum

101 East Court Square (Map 2)
Decatur
404-373-1088
www.dekalbhistory.org
Open: M–F, 9:00 AM–4:00 PM
Admission: Free

Located in the Old Courthouse on the Square, the six rooms of the Dekalb History Museum are chock-full of artifacts, memorabilia, and photographs from 1823 to the present. The museum does a remarkable job celebrating the everyday lives of Dekalb County citizens as they helped the county evolve from a frontier outpost to a bustling community within greater Atlanta. In 1864 General Sherman marched a prong of his invading army mere feet from the Old Courthouse, which is highlighted in two of the museum's rooms dedicated to the role of the county and its citizens in the Civil War.

Highlights:

Biographical information about Dekalb County's grand dame, Mary A. H. Gay. Ms. Gay's memoir *Life in Dixie During the War* helped inspire Margaret Mitchell to write *Gone with the Wind*

Period dresses and a quilt from 1885

Minie balls with teeth marks — Civil War surgeons had their patients bite down on these minie balls before beginning an amputation

Delta Air Transport Heritage Museum

1060 Delta Boulevard (Map 2)
404-715-7886
www.deltamuseum.org
Open: M–F, 9:00 AM–4:00 PM. Please call ahead at least one day
prior to your visit to coordinate your arrival through the Delta headquarters' security.
Admission: Free

Tucked into a hanger at Delta Airlines Worldwide
Headquarters, the Delta Air Transport Heritage Museum celebrates the rich history of Delta Airlines, an Atlanta institution with humble roots. Before transporting passengers, Delta
specialized in crop dusting. In 1929, when it started transporting
passengers, Delta employed ten mechanics. Today it employs
nearly 10,000 technical operators that keep its planes flying.
During the Second World War, the airline's employees played
key roles in training combat pilots and army mechanics. Visitors
to the museum can see a replica of the Monroe, Louisiana, air-
port from which Delta transported its first passengers. Inside
the hanger are three beautifully restored vintage aircraft: a
Stinson SR 8E Reliant, a Curtis Wright Travel Air 6B Sedan,
and a DC3. Each of these aircraft figured prominently during
different periods in the company's history. Other exhibits fea-
ture Delta's technical operations and historical highlights. The
museum also manages an archive that includes photographs and
Delta memorabilia.

Highlights:

A reproduction travel wicker seat used in Delta's aircraft in
1929 sitting next to a modern day electronic business-elite seat

Exhibits dedicated to three former airlines—Northeast, Pan Am, and Western—that were absorbed into modern-day Delta Airlines

Discovering Stone Mountain Museum

Robert E. Lee Boulevard (Map 2)
Stone Mountain Park
770-498-5690
www.stonemountainpark.com
Open: M–F, 9:00 AM–6:00 PM
Admission: Free. To enter Stone Mountain Park, visitors must purchase an $8.00 permit per vehicle.

Larger than Mount Rushmore, the carving on Stone Mountain—billed as the world's largest relief carving—took more than 57 years and three main carvers to complete. The final chips and chisels were completed in 1972. From the towering glass windows in Memorial Hall, the building housing the Discovering Stone Mountain Museum, visitors can get a fantastic view of the carving's three figures: Jefferson Davis, president of the Confederacy during the Civil War; General Robert E. Lee; and Lieutenant General Stonewall Jackson. Upstairs, the museum does an excellent job of tracing the history of Stone Mountain from the Native Americans who first inhabited the site 10,000 years ago to the arrival of white settlers in the 1800s. A large section of the museum is dedicated to the Civil War, and revolvers, swords, and rare rifles are on display. The museum's final exhibits educate visitors on the carving of the mountain as well as remind them that Stone Mountain granite was a much sought-after building material that has been used in projects around the world, including the Capitol Building in Havana, Cuba; the locks of the Panama Canal; the Imperial Hotel in Japan; and the United States Capitol building.

Highlights:

A collection of raptor talons used by Native Americans for jewelry

A large diorama of a Stone Mountain farm from the 1860s

Model showing how massive the general stars are on Robert E. Lee's uniform in the monument

Federal Reserve Bank of Atlanta: Visitors Center & Monetary Museum

1000 Peachtree Street, NE (Map 1)

404-498-8500

www.frbatlanta.org

Open: M–F, 9:00 AM–4:00 PM

Admission: Free

Atlanta is home to one of 12 reserve banks in the United States. This particular building was constructed in 2001 on the main thoroughfare of Peachtree Street, and its presence is intentionally dominating. The bank's appearance, with its solid marble exterior and monolithic Roman architecture, was designed to communicate power and competence and to instill confidence in the American monetary and banking system. This small museum can easily be enjoyed in under an hour. It is surprisingly fun and playful, two words that rarely come to mind when one thinks of banking. Nevertheless, the facility maintains many interactive touch-screen pieces through which the evolution of banking in America is chronicled. A brief history of how and why the Federal Reserve came to be is described, along with a rudimentary explanation of how monetary policy helps guide general economic behavior. The history of money and counterfeiting is explored, with an opportunity for visitors to try their luck at spotting counterfeits. The tour ends in a room with three-sided glass walls. Here, the inner operations of the Fed's cash processing area can be viewed. The cash bus, or robot cars, can be seen continually moving large clear boxes of cash to and from the vault. It is truly amazing how automated the process is!

Highlights:

Free souvenir bags containing actual shredded currency (part of the approximately $13 million the Atlanta Fed destroys daily)

Counterfeit bills on display (You decide what is real or fake.)

Glass window that allows view of the Fed's backroom operations of processing cash; fully automated robot cars shuttling boxes of money back and forth from the printers, the vaults, and the shredders

Fernbank Museum of Natural History

767 Clifton Road (Map 2)

404-929-6300

www.fernbank.edu

Open: M–Sa, 10:00 AM–5:00 PM; Su, noon–5:00 PM

Admission: Adults, $12.00; Seniors and Students, $11.00; Children 3–12, $10.00; Members and Children under 3, free

Atlanta's "Home to the Dinosaurs" is a focal point within the community. Founded in 1938 by Emily Harrison and Dr. Woolford Baker in an attempt to purchase 65 acres of old-growth woodland where Emily had played as a child, the Fernbank now not only preserves this forest but also tells the story of Georgia's unique natural history. The 160,000-square-foot facility opened in 1992 and was the first museum in the world to display the world's largest dinosaur, Argentinosaurus, standing 86 feet tall. There is much to enjoy at the Fernbank, requiring a little choosing and most likely multiple trips back. Permanent exhibits include Giants of the Mesozoic, A Walk Through Time in Georgia, Sensing Nature, Cultures of the World, World of Shells, and First Georgians. In addition, an IMAX theater is also on location with different films throughout the year, generally featuring natural wonders of the world. Of special note is the popular Martinis & IMAX presented every Friday night, January through November (for pricing and other information refer to http://www.fernbank.edu/museum/martinis.html). Enjoy live jazz, food, and drinks before a film. On site are several other permanent features of the center, including the Robert L. Staton Rose Garden, the Children's Discovery Rooms, Fernbank Forest (65 acres), the Star

Gallery, Fossil Floors, and the Naturalist Center (which includes the unique Ask a Geologist resource—visitors can bring in objects for identification by one of the museum's geologists). Many new special exhibits are on display throughout the year. Call or check the Web site before planning a visit.

Fernbank Science Center

156 Heaton Park Drive, NE (Map 2)

678-874-7102

www.fernbanksciencecenter.org

Open: M–F, 8:30 AM–5:00 PM; Th & F –10:00 PM; Sa, 10:00
AM–5:00 PM; Su, 1:00 PM–5:00 PM

Admission: Free except Planetarium: Adults, $4.00; Seniors and
Students, $3.00

The Fernbank Science Center is adjacent to the 65-acre
Fernbank Forest (which is also home to the Fernbank Museum
of Natural History). The center includes the Exhibit Hall,
Planetarium, Observatory, Aerospace Education Laboratory,
Library, Meteorology Lab, and an entrance to the Fernbank
Forest. The Exhibit Hall weaves together nicely the unfolding
story of Georgia's natural history while also highlighting space
exploration and celestial phenomena. An exhibit in the main
wing explores the history of Peachtree Creek as an integral part
of Georgia's past. The exhibit explores how this small tributary
of the greater Chattahoochee contributed to the rapid expansion of Atlanta. Entrepreneurs harnessed the creek's power to
create a bustling milling industry in the mid-1800s. Its early
impact can still be seen in the names of major roads such as
Howell Mill and Moore's Mill, once large mills located on the
banks of Peachtree Creek. There are several smaller exhibits
with displays on the natural inhabitants of the Georgia's various
regions, with particular focus on the coastal and wetland areas.
In addition to exploring Georgia's wildlife, the center also
explores what Georgia was like during the prehistoric era when
dinosaurs roamed the region. Several exhibits are also devoted

to space exploration, the exciting phenomena of the night skies, and the science behind such celestial objects as asteroids and meteors.

Highlights:

The actual Apollo 6 Command Console, part of the last unmanned Apollo mission

Meteor debris, including a piece found from a meteor crash in Odessa, Texas, in 1922

Pictures of different nebulas taken by the famous Hubble and Galileo Space Probe

The Georgia Capitol Museum

431 State Capitol (Map 1)
404-651-6996
Open: M–F, 8:00 AM–5:30 PM
Admission: Free

Housed on the fourth floor of the Georgia Capitol Building,
the Georgia Capitol Museum is a wonderful collection of over
40 large oak display cases capturing many different aspects of
Georgia's amazing past. Showcasing geological samples found
throughout the state, exploring aspects of the Georgia's natural
history, recounting political milestones in the State Assembly,
the Georgia Capitol Museum covers a wide range of interests.
The museum was founded in 1889 when Georgia's General
Assembly reconstituted the office of state geologist, and gave
him the directive "to collect, analyze and classify specimens of
minerals, plants and soils." A year later the governor designated
the fourth floor of the Capitol as temporary quarters to house
the museum. It has remained there, in its "temporary quarters"
for over a hundred years. Architecturally, the Capitol building
itself is worth examining and exploring. Its cornerstone was laid
on September 2, 1885. While wandering its marble hallways,
make sure you stop in the rotunda to see the large oil paintings
of Benjamin Franklin and George Washington. Sharing this
space with these founding fathers are paintings and marble
busts of the Georgians who signed the nation's founding documents and served in the Continental Congress.

Highlights:

Oil paintings and statuary of famous Georgians found
throughout the building

The display of gem stones and minerals unique to Georgia
Two cases of Native American artifacts highlighting Georgia's rich cultural heritage

The Georgia Governor's Mansion

391 West Paces Ferry Road, NW (Map 2)

404-261-1776

www.gov.state.ga.us

Open: Tu–Th, 10:00 AM–11:30 AM

Admission: Free. Reservations required for groups of ten or more.

Designed by Georgia architect A. Thomas Bradbury and completed in 1968, the Georgia Governor's Mansion sits proudly on 18 picturesque acres in northwest Atlanta. The stately house boasts 30 rooms and over 24,000 square feet of living space. Both Jimmy Carter and Zell Miller have called the mansion home while serving as governor of Georgia. Visitors to the Greek revival home are welcomed by greeters stationed throughout the mansion who share the highlights and history of each room. The tour is limited to the first floor of the mansion where the governor receives guests and dignitaries. The second floor of the home is occupied year-round by the current governor and his family. A fascinating aspect of the tour is the story behind the unassuming table and chairs located just off the kitchen at the back of the mansion. Designers purchased the furniture at a Philadelphia auction where it was being sold by Jim Williams of Savannah, Georgia, to pay for his murder trial. The trial of Jim Williams was detailed in the 1994 novel *Midnight in the Garden of Good and Evil*.

Highlights:

A signed first-edition copy of Margaret Mitchell's *Gone With the Wind*

Notable Federal-period furniture located throughout the home

The Hammonds House

503 Peeples Street, SW (Map 1)
404-752-8730
www.hammondshouse.org
Open: Tu–F, 10:00 AM–6:00 PM; Sa & Su, 1:00 PM–5:00 PM
Admission: Adults, $4.00; Seniors, Students, and Children, $2.00;
Members, free

This nineteenth-century Victorian home located in Atlanta's historic West End has been owned by several prominent Atlanta families over the years, including the fabled author Madge Bigham (*Sonny Elephant*). The house is one of the three oldest in the West End and was the site of Atlanta's first kindergarten circa 1911. It was eventually purchased by Dr. Otis T. Hammonds, a prominent black anesthesiologist and art patron. Dr. Hammonds lived here until his death in 1985. He was an avid supporter and collector of African American and Haitian artwork and antiques. After Dr. Hammonds's death, the house and over 250 pieces of art were purchased by Fulton County. In 1988 it opened as an art museum focused on showcasing the work of artists of African descent. The museum houses four to six exhibits a year that showcase a variety of works from its permanent collection as well as touring exhibits. The permanent collection contains pieces from famed artists Romare Bearden, Radcliffe Bailey, and many others. The Hammonds House prides itself on displaying artwork that invokes discussion around past and present social issues. To facilitate this interaction, a resource center containing rare books, articles, and films is on location and available for review by appointment.

The Herndon Home

587 University Place, NW (Map 1)
404-581-9813
www.herndonhome.org
Open: Please call ahead to arrange a guided tour. December holiday tours are especially popular.
Admission: Adults, $5.00; Students, $3.00; Groups of 20 or more, $4.00; Students, $2.00

Described as "an elegant symbol of black achievement," the Herndon Home is a unique and storied mansion listed on the National Register of Historic Places. Owned and operated by the Alonzo F. and Norris B. Herndon Foundation, the 15-room Herndon Home was built by local black craftsmen in the Beaux Arts style for Alonzo Franklin Herndon, Atlanta's first black millionaire. The home was designed by his wife Adrienne and completed in 1910. Born a slave, and forced to sharecrop after the Civil War, Alonzo Herndon had a truly rags-to-riches story. After gaining his freedom, he grew tired of farming and perfected his skills as a barber in Jonesboro. Herndon then used his business acumen to open and operate barbershops around Atlanta. Using income from his barbershops, he acquired real estate, eventually becoming the most successful black property owner in Atlanta. But Herndon was still not finished. His most audacious move was to acquire the company that became the Atlanta Life Insurance Company, which today is the largest black-owned insurance company in America. Touring the Herndon Home gives visitors the opportunity to see the finest furniture and decorations money could buy at the turn of the nineteenth century, which was rarely attainable for African Americans during that time.

The High Museum of Art

1280 Peachtree Street, NE (Map 1)

404-733-4400

www.high.org

Open: Tu & Wed, 10:00 AM–5:00 PM; Thu & Fri, 10:00 AM–8:00 PM; Sat, 10:00 AM–6:00 PM; Su, noon–5:00 PM. Friday Jazz is the third Friday of each month and is open until 10:00 PM.

Admission: Adults, $15.00; Students with ID and Seniors, $12.00; Children 6–17, $10.00; Members and Children under 6, free

The High Museum is an icon within the Atlanta community as well as the entire Southeastern United States. Much more than a traditional museum, the High is Atlanta's center point for exposure and education of the community to the domestic and international world of art. Originally founded by Mrs. Joseph High in 1905, the museum has had several facilities and has enjoyed tremendous growth. Following a plane crash in 1962 that killed 122 prominent Georgia art patrons, the Atlanta Arts Alliance was founded, and money for the construction of the current location was raised through private funds. Designed by Richard Meier, the main building is hailed as one of the ten best works of American architecture of the 1980s. The High collection maintains over 11,000 pieces in American, African, European, decorative, folk, modern, and contemporary arts and photography. While its permanent collection is quite extensive, the High also hosts many renowned international exhibits. Calling or checking the Web site is recommended to find the most recent exhibits on display. The High opened a massive new exhibition space in November 2005. The 177,000 square feet enables the museum to display a broader portion of its permanent collection and to support special exhibits.

Highlights:

Friday Night Jazz on the third Friday of every month. Cocktails, dinner, and dessert can be enjoyed while listening to local jazz artists

The permanent collection contains pieces from famed artists such as Claude Monet, Jan Brueghel the Elder, Camille Pissarro, Henry Ossawa Tanner, and Romare Bearden

Historic Roswell Visitors Center

617 Atlanta Street (Map 4)
Roswell
770-640-3253
www.cvb.roswell.ga.us
Open: M–F, 9:00 AM–5:00 PM; Sa, 10:00 AM–4:00 PM; Su,
noon–3:00 PM
Admission: Free

The city of Roswell was established as a result of its proximity
to the Chattahoochee River. Vickery Creek, which feeds into
the nearby river provided the necessary power to create an
industrial base that by the mid-1850s had become the largest in
North Georgia. Roswell King built the first cotton mill in
what is now historic Roswell. Perhaps the mill's most notorious
output, before being burned by Union general W. T. Sherman
during his siege of Atlanta, was Roswell Gray, which was
material used for Confederate uniforms. The visitors center is
located only one block away from this famous mill and was
once the mill's company store, selling provisions to its employees. The visitors center is staffed by local history enthusiasts
who are all too happy to discuss local folklore and popular sites.
If you are planning to take in historic Roswell, this center is a
quick must-see. They have videos, books, and brochures on all
of the surrounding historic sites. In addition, they have a small
collection of historic artifacts that were uncovered in the area
and a few dioramas of the historic district.

Imagine It! Children's Museum

275 Centennial Olympic Park Drive, NW (corner of Baker Street; Map 1)
404-659-KIDS (5437)
www.imagineit-cma.org
Open: M–F, 10:00 AM–4:00 PM; Sa & Su, 10:00 AM–5:00 PM
Admission: Adults and Children over 3, $11.00

Imagine It! was created in the early 1990s and resides across from Atlanta's beautiful Centennial Olympic Park. It was the city's response to being the only major city without a children's museum. Although late in coming, the museum's creators made good use of adapting the best ideas from other cities' exhibits. Created for children under the age of eight, the museum operates a "touch everything" philosophy in which children are encouraged to play, explore, learn, and interact. It is divided into five main exhibits, including a giant interactive mechanical ball machine, fishing pond, an area for wall painting, a dance and music area, and a miniature grocery store. The museum has become quite popular with local families. While the museum has many fun activities to enjoy in its exhibits, they also bring in musicians, storytellers, actors, and artists to perform for the children. This is a must-see for anyone with children. You won't be disappointed! Capacity is limited and fills up fast, it is recommended to always purchase tickets ahead of time (for a specific time). Memberships are also available and quite popular; refer to the Web site for prices.

Highlights:

An interactive mechanical ball machine reminiscent of an apparatus straight out of *Willy Wonka & the Chocolate Factory*

A giant splash and fishing pond for children

The Kennesaw Depot Museum

2829 Cherokee Street (Map 3)
Kennesaw
770-975-0877
Open: M–F, 9:00 AM–5:00 PM
Admission: Free

Just as the city of Atlanta traces its origins to the arrival rail-roads in Georgia, Kennesaw's past is similarly linked to the rails. Originally named Big Shanty for the worker shanties that sprang up along the newly laid tracks in the late 1840s, Kennesaw was put on the map during the Civil War. General Sherman launched his infamous March to the Sea by destroy-ing the railroads linking Kennesaw to Atlanta. Today visitors can enjoy a slice of Kennesaw's history at the Kennesaw Depot Museum, which occupies a small railroad depot. The museum, which opened in 2001, is located across the street from the Southern Museum of Civil War and Locomotive History. The Kennesaw Depot Museum's features concise exhibits on Kennesaw History, the Cherokee Nation, the Civil War, and the Glover Machine Works, which started manufacturing steam-powered locomotives in the late 1800s. The self-guided tour through the depot is quick, easy, and informative.

Kennesaw National Battlefield Park & Museum

905 Kennesaw Mountain Drive (Map 3)

Kennesaw

770-427-4686

www.nps.gov/kemo/

Open: Daily, 8:30 AM–5:00 PM

Admission: Free. Optional shuttle bus: Adults, $2.00; Children 6–12, $1.00; Children under 6, free

The battlefield's museum offers a brief overview of the Civil War for novices, but exhibits focus more on the individual generals, politicians, and the political climate at the time of the famous Atlanta Campaign of 1864. The museum reveals that both the Union and Confederacy considered winning a decisive battle to be of vital importance during the reelection campaign of Abraham Lincoln. The Union army delivered such a blow to the South through the Atlanta Campaign. While the museum documents the history of this famous Civil War battleground, the landscape and the recreation opportunities of this beautiful region also provide enjoyment. This is a very popular site among the locals for hiking and picnicking on nice afternoons. There are four major battle sites that are of note: Kennesaw Mountain, Pigeon Hill, Cheatham Hill, and Kolb's Farm. Check the Web site before visiting due to changing educational opportunities being offered.

Highlights:

Occasional battle reenactments and costumed Civil War soldiers explaining common weaponry and tactics

Extensive walking and jogging trails. (Leashed dogs allowed.)

The King Center

Freedom Hall
449 Auburn Avenue, NE (Map 1)
404-526-8923
www.thekingcenter.org
Open: M–Su, 9:00 AM–5:00 PM; 9:00 AM–6:00 PM (Memorial Day to
Labor Day)
Admission: Free; Donations welcome

Maintained by the King family, the King Center contains a
three-room gallery with exhibits on Rosa Parks; the lives of
Martin Luther King, Jr., and Corretta Scott King; and King's
visit to India in 1959. As the primary spokesman and leader of
the Civil Rights movement from 1955 to 1968, Martin Luther
King, Jr., epitomized the larger-than-life persona of an epochal
leader. The items on display in the King Center offer a
reminder that he was a flesh-and-blood person. The exhibit
includes everyday items, such as the travel alarm clock that
woke him up every morning. Visitors can also see the robes he
wore during church services, the denim jacket he wore while
leading marches, and the suit he was wearing when he was
stabbed on September 20, 1958. In the same room are memorabilia from Coretta Scott King's travels to different nations and
a time line of her life. The Rosa Parks room contains black-
and-white photographs of her extended family as well as pictures of her with Martin Luther King, Jr., and Coretta Scott
King during the 1960s. The final room of the gallery educates
visitors on King's inspiration for his nonviolent approach to
racial equality: Mahatma Gandhi. In his first book, *Stride
Toward Freedom*, King gives credit to Gandhi for providing the
inspiration for the Montgomery bus boycott of the 1950s.

Highlights:

A Grammy Award for the Best Spoken Word Recording given posthumously in 1970 for King's speech "Why I Oppose the War in Vietnam"

The key to room 307 at the Lorraine Motel in Memphis, where King was assassinated

Quotes from Gandhi that inspired King's belief in the power of nonviolent resistance

Margaret Mitchell House & Museum

990 Peachtree Street (Map 1)

404-249-7015

www.gwtw.org

Open: M–Su, 9:30 AM–5:00 PM

Admission: Adults, $12.00; Seniors and Students, $9.00; Children 6–17, $5.00; Groups of ten or more, discounts available; Members, free

The Margaret Mitchell House & Museum sets a context for the famed novel *Gone with the Wind* by exploring Mitchell's life, family history, and early career as a journalist. Second in sales only to the Bible, her Pulitzer Prize–winning novel was truly a phenomenon in the way it touched people's lives all around the world. The tour begins in the adjacent visitors center, with a small theater and visual arts exhibit largely displaying Mitchell's work as a journalist for the *Atlanta Journal & Constitution*. The Gone With the Wind Movie Museum follows, showcasing various movie memorabilia and providing a look at the movie's dramatic social impact. The tour continues to the famed Apartment #1 of what was once known as the Crescent Apartments, where Mitchell and her husband lived as she wrote the novel from 1925 to 1932. The apartment is furnished as it would have been during this time and offers insight into Mitchell's wild, young spirit. Of note is the lion's head on the staircase banister that Mitchell rubbed for good luck every time she entered the house and was rendered in the movie during the scene in which Scarlett O'Hara falls down the stairs. The top two floors of the building were twice burned by arsonists in the 1990s, but the building was restored to its original condition through a donation of Daimler-Benz. The house is a literary landmark — a symbol of old Midtown — and houses the Center for Southern Literature.

For *Gone With the Wind* enthusiasts, we recommend purchasing the Premiere Pass, which includes five separate attractions: Atlanta Cyclorama and Civil War Museum, Historical & Hysterical Tours (costumed guided car tour to various locations in Jonesboro, GA), Margaret Mitchell House, Road to Tara Museum, and Stately Oaks Plantation.

Highlights:

Memorabilia from the movie filming, including set sketches, costumes, and telegrams in which the famed actors accepted their roles

Tour guides who provide a clear context for the change of Atlanta from the postbellum period to today

The tiny apartment, which Mitchell affectionately called "the dump," where she lived on Peachtree Street while writing the novel

Marietta Gone with the Wind Museum: Scarlett on the Square

18 Whitlock Avenue (Map 3)

Marietta

770-794-5576

www.gwtwmarietta.com

Open: M–Sa, 10:00 AM–5:00 PM

Admission: Adults, $7.00; Seniors and Students, $6.00; Groups of 15 or more, $5.00

For any *Gone with the Wind* enthusiast, this museum is a must-see. Established in 2003, the museum is located in historic Marietta Square in the nineteenth-century Old Thomas Wharehouse building. It houses Dr. Christopher Sullivan's personal collection of Gone with the Wind movie and novel memorabilia. A large portion of this museum is dedicated to an exhibit that showcases scores of internationally bootlegged copies of Margaret Mitchell's famed novel. In fact, Mitchell only wrote one book, but she spent much of the rest of her life fighting the international copyright infringements that the books on display represent. This exhibit is essentially a testament to her struggles against the volumes of bootlegged novels from a variety of countries. The collection also provides a behind the scenes look at the making of the film with actual photographs, set drawings, and telegrams between the actors and the director. A few of the actual costumes worn by Vivien Leigh are on display. The gift shop is an additional point of interest, with all sorts of *Gone with the Wind* items, including china place settings, music boxes, T-shirts, and more.

Marietta Museum of History

1 Depot Street, Suite 200 (Map 3)
Marietta
770-528-0431
www.mariettahistory.org
Open: M–Su, 10:00 AM–4:00 PM
Admission: Adults, $3.00; Seniors and Students, $2.00; Children under 6 and Members, free

The Marietta Museum of History is located on the second and third floor of the Kennesaw House, a block away from historic Marietta Square. The Kennesaw House has historic significance itself in that it served as a Confederate hospital and morgue, and Andrew's raiders occupied a room here the night before their daring theft of the steam engine the *General*. The museum focuses on the growth of Marietta and Cobb County beginning with the original Native Americans. Additional exhibits include a Civil War gallery and artifacts from all major American conflicts. The exhibits can easily be enjoyed in under an hour, leaving time to further explore historic Marietta Square. There are many attractions in the square, including cafés, antiques shops, and theaters. In addition, there are a number of historic antebellum homes just off the square that can be viewed along Kennesaw Avenue, which runs from the Square to Kennesaw Mountain.

Highlights:
A small Civil War exhibit located in the very room that Andrew's raiders spent the night before their famous locomotive theft
Extensive gun and camera collections on the third floor

Marietta/Cobb Museum of Art

30 Atlanta Street (Map 3)
Marietta
770-528-1444
www.mariettasquare.com/mcma
Open: Tu–F, 11:00 AM–5:00 PM; Sa, 11:00 AM–4:00 PM; Su, 1:00
PM–5:00 PM. Closed between exhibits.
Admission: Adults, $5.00; Seniors and Students, $3.00; Children under
6 and Members, free

The Marietta Cobb Museum of Art is located off historic
Marietta Square in a beautifully renovated Greek Revival
building that was originally constructed in 1910 as the Cobb
County post office. The museum prides itself on being the
only Atlanta metropolitan museum focused solely on
American art. The museum maintains collections of various
nineteenth- and twentieth-century American artists, including
Andy Warhol and Andrew Wyeth. However, depending on
the current exhibit size, none of the permanent collection may
be on display. Therefore, we recommend calling ahead before
visiting the museum.

Martin Luther King, Jr., National Historic Site

501 Auburn Avenue, NE (Map 1)

404-331-5198, ext. 3017

www.nps.gov/malu

Open: M–Su, 9:00 AM–5:00 PM; M–Su, 9:00 AM–6:00 PM (Jun. 15–Aug. 15)

Admission: Free; Donations welcome

The consortium of facilities and historic houses that make up the Martin Luther King, Jr., Historic Site honors the life and accomplishments of one of America's greatest social activists. Beginning with a tour of the birth home, visitors can see the bedroom where Martin Luther King, Jr., and his two siblings were born. Surrounding the birth home are period homes as well as shotgun shacks dating from Dr. King's childhood. Tours begin in the oldest standing firehouse in Atlanta, which is located on the same block. Two streets down from the birth home is the historic Ebenezer Baptist Church where Dr. King honed his skills as an orator. When religious services are not in session, visitors can sit in the church pews, view the stained glass windows containing names of original parishioners, and listen to audio of Dr. King's greatest speeches. Across the street from Ebenezer Baptist Church is the visitors center containing a poignant 15-minute film about the life and accomplishments of Dr. King. Along with the film is a thought-provoking children's exhibit about the reach and scope of discrimination facing African Americans in the years leading up to the Civil Rights movement of the 1960s.

Highlights:

The reflecting pool surrounding Dr. King's tomb

The bedroom Dr. King shared with his brother as a young boy

An original audio recording of Dr. King calling for racial equality through nonviolence

Michael C. Carlos Museum at Emory University

571 South Kilgo Circle (Map 2)

404-727-4282

www.carlos.emory.edu

Open: Tu–Sa, 10:00 AM–5:00 PM; Su, noon–5:00 PM. Closed university holidays.

Admission: Suggested donation, $7.00; Emory University Students and Faculty, free

Located on the picturesque campus of Emory University, the Carlos Museum maintains the largest collection of ancient art in the Southeast. It is filled with objects from Egypt, Greece, Rome, the Near East, and Pre-Columbian America. In addition to these remarkable holdings, the museum is also home to collections of sub-Saharan African art as well as European and American woodcuttings and sketches. The Carlos Museum traces its history to 1920 when Emory professor William Shelton traveled to Egypt with the American Scientific Mission and began acquiring artifacts for the university. In 1999 the museum electrified the city of Atlanta with the purchase of a collection of Egyptian antiquities from a private museum in Niagara Falls, Canada, that greatly increased its holdings.

Highlights:

Richly decorated coffins and coffin boards as well as mummies from ancient Egypt

Pottery from all three principal cultural centers of the Americas: Mesoamerica, Central America, and the Andes

The versatility of ancient Greek craftsmen as demonstrated by the remarkable breadth of the media in which they worked, including gold, silver, electrum, bronze, lead, ivory, bone, marble, semiprecious stones, glass, and clay

Museum of Contemporary Art (MOCA)

1447 Peachtree Street (Map 1)
404-881-1109
www.mocaga.org
Open: Tu–Sa, 10:00 AM–5:00 PM
Admission: Free; Donations welcome

Tucked away in a small commercial space on Peachtree Street in Midtown, this gem of a museum is something you might miss if you aren't paying attention. On the first floor of the building is a small, but intriguing, three-room gallery. MOCA's mission is to serve as an exhibition home and an educational facility for Georgia artists. In addition, approximately eight national and international exhibits are featured each year. MOCA was established in 1994 with private money and a private collection from David Golden, president of the real estate advisory firm CGR Advisors. The museum prides itself on its continued focus to archive and preserve a private collection of pieces created as early as the 1940s. Over 275 works have been collected and archived there from over 125 artists from the state of Georgia. Although contemporary, the art collection spans media ranging from folk art to digital prints. It's the perfect museum to enjoy the work of Georgia artists while on a lunch break.

Highlights:
A magnificent range of contemporary pieces highlighting many styles and disciplines

Museum of Design Atlanta

285 Peachtree Center Avenue (Map 1)
404-979-6455
www.museumofdesign.org
Open: Tu–Sa, 11:00 AM–5:00 PM
Admission: Free

Utilizing three spacious exhibition spaces located on the lobby and garden levels of the Marquis II Office Tower, the Museum of Design Atlanta (MODA) offers visitors a respite from the hustle and bustle of downtown Atlanta. Incorporated in 1989 and officially named an affiliate of the prestigious Smithsonian Institution, MODA's mission is to "explore the impact of design on our daily lives." MODA occupies a unique niche as one of only a handful of museums in the United States dedicated exclusively to design. While walking through its exhibits, visitors are confronted with the question "Should the design of everyday objects—dishes, furniture, light fixtures—be considered art?" Through its partnership with the Smithsonian, MODA is able to bring impressive collections to Atlanta honoring the emphasis of its founders Jon Eric Riis and Richard Mafong. The two visionaries created MODA "to promote a better appreciation and understanding of the peoples of the world through examination of a society's art and design, both past and present, and the influences upon it over time."

The Museum of the Jimmy Carter Library

441 Freedom Parkway (Map 1)
404-865-7100
www.jimmycarterlibrary.org
Open: M–Sa, 9:00 AM–4:45 PM; Su, noon–4:45 PM
Admission: Adults, $8.00; Seniors, Students, and Military, $6.00;
Children under 17, free

The Jimmy Carter library and museum is part of the presidential library system and focuses on the key issues of Carter's presidency. The center is located on a beautifully landscaped campus in downtown Atlanta that includes a Japanese garden. Upon entering the museum, visitors can view a 20-minute film entitled The Presidency, which focuses on the office, its evolution, and its current power. Upon exiting the film hall, visitors face a wall that features presidents of the twentieth century and the key issues they faced. Just past this hall is a replica of the Oval Office as it was during the Carter administration. A commentary by Jimmy Carter guides visitors, as it explains the meaning of the furniture as well as the unique experiences that the former president remembers taking place there. Jimmy Carter's term as president is largely remembered as a time of international humanitarian outreach, and the museum is a testament to his and the First Lady's efforts. Other exhibits tell the story of the major issues during his term like the Iran Hostage situation, the Camp David Accords, the Panama Canal Treaty, and the formal recognition of the People's Republic of China. While providing a historical backdrop for the events, the museum also displays Jimmy Carter's notes and memos for events, which gives a personal touch to these significant public policy issues. Some of the exhibits allow the viewers to interactively choose how they might have acted in the president's place. Other areas of the museum are dedicated to the history of the Carter family, President Carter's short but meaningful political career from small town Georgia to the White House, his presidential campaign, and a Town Hall–style video question-and-answer session.

Highlights:

Jimmy Carter's Nobel Peace Prize

Many artifacts from his presidential campaign, including Peanut Brigade jerseys, buttons, and bumper stickers

A handwritten speech for the acceptance of the Democratic National Convention presidential nomination

National Museum of Patriotism

1405 Spring Street, NW (corner of 18th Street; Map 1)
404-875-0691
www.museumofpatriotism.org
Open: Tu–Th, Sa & Su, 10:00 AM–4:00 PM
Admission: Adults, $12.00; Seniors and Students 7–18, $6.00;
Children under 6 and members of law enforcement, public safety,
emergency medical services, and active-duty military, free

What is patriotism? The museum answers this question
through an exploration of the history of American patriots—
immigrants, soldiers, and common citizens. A brief video of
America's most significant moments sets the tone for the rest
of the museum. It is hard not to be moved as you walk through
the exhibits, witnessing how countless Americans have sacri-
ficed for their country. The museum was opened in 2004 and
largely works with schools in the area to educate youth. It
showcases a collection of small exhibits focusing on the history
of each branch of the military, American symbols, immigration
as a definition of American culture, and a memorial to the
September 11 terrorist attacks. The true beauty of this museum
is less in its exhibits than in the great pride that is inspired by
celebrating American history.

Highlights:
Trench Art—a collection of actual pieces created by soldiers at
war, such as cigarette lighters made from bullets
A 1945 fully restored Jeep, which you are encouraged to climb
into for a photo

Several thousand Sweetheart Pins, popular during the Second World War, as they gave those at home a way to honor their loved ones

USO: Project Video Connect, which allows visitors to send a video e-mail to military service members all over the world

Oakland Cemetery

248 Oakland Avenue, SE (Map 1)

404-688-2107

www.oaklandcemetery.com

Open: Tours Sa, 10:00 AM & 2:00 PM; Su, 2:00 PM

Admission: Adults, $10.00; Seniors, $3.00; Students and Children over 5, $5.00; Self-guided tour, $2.00. Call or check the Web site for group and family rates.

For the serious student of Atlanta history, the Oakland Cemetery has it all. Set on a remarkable 88 acres a mere mile from city hall, Oakland Cemetery was originally built "in the country" in 1850 at a time when Atlanta was a sleepy railroad town. Burials soon outgrew the original six acres and continued through the 1880s before the cemetery ran out of space. Remarkably, over 70,000 people are buried in Oakland, including 6,000 Confederate soldiers, 17,000 African Americans, and a large percentage of Atlanta's early Jewish population. Famous Atlantans such as author Margaret Mitchell, golfer Bobby Jones, Mayor Maynard Jackson, and the founder of Rich's Department Stores, Emanuel Rich, are all buried at Oakland. The cemetery's Victorian tombstones and mausoleums make it a mecca for both professional and amateur photographers. Today it is the third largest green space in the city. Guided tours are highly recommended.

Highlights:

The Victorian-era symbolism found on tombstones throughout the cemetery

A Confederate soldier's tombstone inscribed with a single name: Batman

The contrast between the different ethnicities and religions of those interred at Oakland

Oglethorpe Museum of Art

4484 Peachtree Road, NE (Map 2)
(3rd Floor of the Philip Weltner Library building on campus)
404-364-8555
http://museum.oglethorpe.edu
Open: Th–Su, noon–5:00 PM. Closed Mondays and university holidays.
Admission: Adults, $5.00; Children under 12, free

Named after the founder of Georgia, James Edward Oglethorpe, Oglethorpe University was founded in 1835 as a southern institution for training Presbyterian ministers. The university closed it doors twice—once at the outbreak of the Civil War and again due to its struggles during the Reconstruction era—before being rechartered and relocated to northern Atlanta in 1913. The gothic revival architecture style is a tribute to Oglethorpe's alma mater, Oxford. Touted as the only small liberal-arts university museum in the southeast, the Oglethorpe Museum of Art generally showcases three international exhibits a year and augments these with its own impressive permanent collection. There are two spacious yet quaint galleries, which are located on the third floor of the Philip Weltner University Library building. The permanent collection consists of a variety of works, including sculptures, paintings, photography, and prints. The paintings are of several contemporary realism painters, including Richard Maury, Jeffery Mims, Richard Serin, and Francisco Roa. The museum is quite active within the Atlanta art community and frequently features speakers. Please call ahead for current exhibits and guest speakers.

Rhodes Hall: The Castle on Peachtree Street

1516 Peachtree Street, NW (Map 1)

404-885-7800

www.georgiatrust.org/historic_sites/rhtourinfo.htm

Open: M–F, 11:00 AM–4:00 PM; Su, noon–3:00 PM; Behind-the-scenes tour, Su only

Admission: Adults, $5.00; Seniors and Students, $4.00; Georgia Trust Members, free; Group rates available; Behind-the-scenes tour, $8.00

Amos Giles Rhodes, founder of Rhodes Furniture Company, was one of the New South's and Atlanta's most successful entrepreneurs. A man of modest means, he arrived in Atlanta in 1875 from Kentucky and built a thriving business, which sold moderately priced furniture on credit at a time when most homes had been destroyed by Sherman's March to the Sea. The castle was built between 1902 and 1904 and was born out of Rhode's obsession with the medieval architecture he found along Germany's Rhine River. During this time period, many antebellum estates could be found up and down this section of Peachtree Street. The exterior structure is constructed of solid granite from Atlanta's famed Stone Mountain. The interior showcases an Italian Renaissance–inspired dining room and eighteenth-century French ladies' parlor. Each room is an architectural masterpiece; the interior was known as one of the most technologically sophisticated of its time, equipped with electric lights, steam furnaces, and electric servant bells. The Georgia Trust, which oversees the protection of Georgia's historic resources, operates an office on the second and third floors of the building. Tours of those levels as well as of the tower are only available during the behind-the-scenes tours on Sunday afternoons. This fabulous structure is also available to rent out for corporate or family events and is quite affordable.

Highlights:

A series of beautifully painted stained glass pieces depicting the major events in the Civil War

Road to Tara Museum

104 N. Main Street (Map 2)

Jonesboro

770-478-4800

www.visitscarlett.com

Open: M–F, 8:30 AM–5:00 PM; Sa, 10:00 AM–4:00 PM

Admission: Adults, $5.00; Seniors and Students, $4.00

The Road to Tara Museum is located in downtown historic Jonesboro (approximately 15 miles south of downtown Atlanta) at the Jonesboro Depot Welcome Center. The depot was originally constructed in 1867 in a small town south of Jonesboro but relocated in 1880 to support the rail line between Marthasville (now Atlanta), Savannah, and Forsyth. During the Battle of Jonesboro, the depot was burned by General Kilpatrick, as the station was vital for transporting supplies throughout the South. The museum has an excellent collection of movie artifacts, actor and actress signatures, and personal effects of Margaret Mitchell. Of particular interest, however, is the relationship between Jonesboro and *Gone with the Wind*. It has been long believed that Tara, Scarlett O'Hara's family plantation home, was based upon Stately Oaks Plantation (*see below*) in present-day Jonesboro. In fact, Jonesboro legally obtained the right to be labeled "home of *Gone with the Wind*" from Stephen Mitchell, Margaret's brother. There are several pieces in the museum that help explain the connection between Jonesboro, Margaret Mitchell, and *Gone with the Wind*. Although called the Road to Tara Museum, the museum spends an equal amount of space explaining the significance of the Battle of Jonesboro. This battle occurred near the end of the Atlanta campaign and sealed the fated of the Confederacy when Atlanta's supply lines were cut off. The exhibit portrays the lives of several soldiers and their fight to defend their homes. The museum also displays a number of Civil War artifacts that were found in the area such a Bible, a pocket watch, a wallet, a shaving kit, and bullets.

For *Gone With the Wind* enthusiasts, we recommend purchasing the Premiere Pass, which includes five separate attractions: Atlanta Cyclorama and Civil War Museum, Historical & Hysterical Tours (costumed guided car tour to various locations in Jonesboro, GA), Margaret Mitchell House, Road to Tara Museum, and Stately Oaks Plantation.

Highlights:

The Train Depot, which has had two more recent brushes with fame: the 1970s rock band Lynard Skynard shot the cover of their first album outside, and it was featured in the 1977 film *Smokey and the Bandit*

A real Sherman Necktie: the bent train-track rails that were left in the wake of the Union forces after they dismantled Confederate rail lines

A variety of actual photos of the city of Atlanta prior to Sherman's siege

Robert C. Williams American Museum of Papermaking

500 10th Street, NW (Map 1)

404-894-5700

www.ipst.gatech.edu/amp/index.html

Open: M–F, 9:00 AM–5:00 PM. Closed university holidays.

Admission: Free

Located on the first floor of the Institute of Paper Science and Technology at Georgia Tech, the Robert C. Williams American Museum of Papermaking offers a wide-ranging and fascinating look at the origins and global spread of one of the most common objects in our daily lives: paper. The museum begins with the history of the first paper mill in Georgia, which was located at Scull Shoals on the Oconee River. Built in 1811 by Zachariah Sims, the mill supplied paper to three Georgia newspapers: the Athens Gazette, the Foreign Correspondent, and the Georgia Express. The word "paper" is derived from the word "papyrus," which was a plant on which the ancient Egyptians began writing 5,000 years ago. However, it was a Chinese government official, Ts'ai Lun, who is credited with inventing paper in AD 105. The museum has a myriad of exhibits showing that before Ts'ai Lun invented paper, societies from around the world found interesting ways to record their histories and commerce. In addition to the papyrus plant, people used beaten bark, tree leaves, and sheepskins to record important details about their lives and communities. The final section of the museum explores the role technology has played in the commercialization of papermaking.

Highlights:

The story of the spread of paper from China to Korea, Japan, and Europe

Ancient papermaking tools used by different cultures

Examples of intricate watermarks stamped into highest-quality paper

Root House Museum

4 Depot Street (Map 3)
Marietta
770-426-4982
www.cobblandmarks.com
Open: Tu–Sa, 11:00 AM–4:00 PM
Admission: Adults, $4.00; Seniors, $3.00; Children, $2.00

Located just off Marietta Square, the Root House is one of the oldest remaining wooden-frame homes constructed in Marietta. The house was built around 1845 by Hannah and William Root. William was one of the earliest known merchants in Marietta and its first druggist. The house was moved two blocks from its original site, and it has been renovated with great care. Although not nearly as glamorous as most plantation homes on display in the area, the Root House is much more typical of a middle class family in Atlanta prior to the Civil War. The home furnishings are not the originals, but a collection of authentic period pieces have been assembled, creating a look and feel similar to the Roots' original household. The grounds also contain a separate privy, kitchen house, and garden. A personally guided tour through this museum is perfect for children and antique lovers.

The Roswell Fire and Rescue Museum

1002 Alpharetta Street (Map 4)

Roswell

770-641-3730

Open: M–Su, 9:00 AM–7:00 PM. Museum closed when rescue workers respond to fire or EMS incident.

Admission: Free

Housed in the same complex as Roswell Fire Department Station #1, the two rooms of the museum display antique fire nozzles, axes, canvas buckets, and brass bells to highlight the progress made in firefighting techniques. Throughout the museum, memorabilia and objects celebrate the history of Roswell's fire and rescue units. The museum also has an interesting collection of fire marks. Residents of early American cities displayed fire marks—plaques made of wood or metal—on the outside of their homes based on their affiliation with a fire insurance company. If a fire engulfed a house and a rival fire brigade with a different insurance company arrived on the scene, it had no obligation to extinguish the fire.

Highlights:

A fully restored, red 1947 Ford LaFrance pumper truck

Panoramic photos of the destruction caused by Atlanta's Great Fire of 1917 that burned 73 city blocks and destroyed 1,553 homes

A wooden rattle used by night watchmen in the eighteenth century to alert sleeping residents to a neighborhood fire

Roswell Walking Tours by the Roswell Historical Society

617 Atlanta Street (Map 4)

Roswell

770-992-1665

www.cvb.roswell.ga.us

Open: W, 10:00 AM–?; Sa, 1:00 PM–?

Admission: $5.00

Many of the homes in historic Roswell survived a siege by Union troops during the Civil War, preserving many interesting tales and stories. The walking tour through historic Roswell is an hour and a half of the excellent oral history and folklore related to these houses. The tours are led by local history enthusiasts who are familiar with the stories behind every building in the area. The town, founded by Roswell King, became a popular retreat for the Georgia aristocracy seeking an escape from the oppressive coastal summers. The tours' stories largely focus on the extraordinary events that surrounded this mill town beginning in July of 1864. After the Battle of Kennesaw Mountain, General Sherman was looking for a way to cross the Chattahoochee River. He sent an advance cavalry division to capture Roswell, a small town on the northern banks of the river. Many of the buildings seen along the tour have individual stories of being seized by Union troops. Of particular interest is the tale of the Roswell Mill, which was burned to the ground after its French manager attempted to pass the business off as a French institution to save it from seizure. Upon learning the truth, the infuriated Union General ordered the mill burned and deported nearly 700 women workers north.

Highlights:

The Presbyterian Church—built in 1840 and used as a hospital by Union troops

Great Oaks—Reverend Nathaniel Pratt's home (pastor of the Presbyterian Church), which became a Union barracks and headquarters

Mimosa Hall—owned by John Dunwoody and used as a Union hospital

The Salvation Army Southern Historical Center and Museum

1032 Metropolitan Parkway, SW (Map 1)
404-752-7578
www.salvationarmysouth.org/museum
Open: M–F, 9:00 AM–noon & 1:00 PM–4:00 PM; Call ahead for guided tours for groups of five or more.
Admission: Free; Donations welcome

An icon of global service that is recognized throughout the world, the Salvation Army has a rich and colorful history that is brought to life in the museum located on the Atlanta campus of the Salvation Army's College for Officer Training. The museum, which encompasses 3,700 square feet, guides visitors through the founding of the Salvation Army in England by William and Catherine Booth in 1865 to its arrival in the United States in the late 1880s. One of the first exhibits explains how the Salvation Army's commitment to United States servicemen during the First World War earned widespread gratitude from the soldiers' families, which ultimately endeared the organization to the American public. Visitors are then treated to Colonel Dick Norris' collection of memorabilia, which displays the various posters, postcards, and publications that helped publicize the Salvation Army in the United States. The final exhibits of the museum focus on the history and achievements of the Salvation Army's Southern Territory and educate visitors on the outreach programs—original musical compositions, work therapy at its thrift stores, disaster services, creation of the USO (United Service Organization), which supports the United States armed forces—that have made the Salvation Army a household name. The Salvation Army Southern Historical Center and Museum chronicles a story of service and outreach. The organization's archives contain original documents and photographs for the serious scholar. The facility is one of the hidden jewels of Atlanta's cultural landscape.

Highlights:

An entire wall containing the museum's international postage stamp collection that depicts Salvation Army themes and images

A reconstructed early storefront Salvation Army working space that functioned as a worship hall as well as a service center for community outreach

Smyrna Museum

2868 Atlanta Road (Map 3)
Smyrna
770-431-2858
Open: M–Sa, 10:00 AM–4:00 PM
Admission: Free

The Smyrna Museum's exterior is a replica of the original train station in Smyrna that was built in the early 1800s. The museum tells the evolving story of Smyrna, or Camp Smyrna as it was originally called. The town was founded as a training site for the Georgia militia at the beginning of the Civil War. The Battle of Smyrna (more appropriately titled a skirmish) also took place near the site of the current museum shortly after the famous Battle of Kennesaw Mountain. The museum contains a variety of artifacts from different periods of Smyrna's history. Next door to the museum is a replica of Aunt Fanny's Cabin. This was a very popular restaurant and tourist site in Smyrna from 1941 to 1992. It represented the Old South in its famed cooking and hospitality.

Highlights:
Numerous Civil War artifacts found in the area, including an artillery shell that was discoverd, and disarmed, in 1998 by a local plumber who was working at a nearby apartment complex
A replica of Aunt Fanny's Cabin; books for sale featuring her recipes

Southeastern Railway Museum

3595 Peachtree Road (Map 4)

770-476-2013

www.srmduluth.org

Open: F–Su, 10:00 AM–5:00 PM (Apr.–Dec.); Sa, 10:00 AM–5:00 PM (Jan.–Mar.)

Admission: Adults, $7.00; Seniors, $5.00; Children 2–12, $4.00; Children under 2, free

Atlanta can thank the arrival of the railroad in 1845 for its status today as a world-class metropolis. Initially the sleepy town that grew into Atlanta was named Terminus because it represented the southernmost stop on a rail line serving the interior of Georgia. Eventually eight railroad lines would serve the city, bringing economic opportunity and explosive population growth. Today the Southeastern Railway Museum is dedicated to preserving, restoring, and operating "historically significant railway equipment" and introducing visitors to the locomotives and rail cars that built Atlanta. Young and old will enjoy the variety of train cars on display, including locomotives, freight cars, and cabooses from different time periods.

Highlights:

On-site train rides (Call ahead for details.)

The private Pullman car *Superb*, which was used by President Warren Harding in 1923 on a tour of the West and Pacific Northwest

A restored 1910 steam locomotive that was used to make runs between Miami and the Florida Keys

Southern Museum of Civil War & Locomotive History

2829 Cherokee Street (Map 3)

Kennesaw

770-427-2117

www.southernmuseum.org

Open: M–Sa, 9:30 AM–5:00 PM; Su, noon–5:00 PM

Admission: Adults, $7.50; Seniors, $6.50; Children 4–12, $5.50; Children under 4, free

Originally two separate museums, these two collections have been masterfully woven into one family-oriented exhibit affiliated with the Smithsonian Institute. Because the American Civil War was the first war fought utilizing a rail system, the museum focuses largely on the manner in which both armies depended on this rapidly expanding logistical network and how it enabled either side to quickly gain an edge in the brutal conflict. The museum has acquired an impressive collection of Civil War memorabilia, including uniforms, musical instruments, surgeon kits, rifles and pistols, as well as family pictures, letters, and other personal items. The next section of the museum details the history of railroads in the United States. Prominently featured are the members of the Glover Family, who helped to industrialize the war-torn South. The family owned a locomotive manufacturing plant, Glover Machine Works, which is a highlight of the tour. The museum ends with an exciting story about the Big Shanty, as Kennesaw was known during the Civil War. This was the starting point of what many call "the most daring undertaking the Yankees ever planned or attempted." Follow the exciting adventure of a small band of Union soldiers that hijacked the Confederate locomotive the *General*. An amazing chase unfolded from Big Shanty nearly to Chattanooga, resulting in several Union soldiers becoming the first recipients of the Congressional Medal of Honor. This brilliant locomotive is fully restored and on display here.

Highlights:

Many Civil War artifacts, including a Union cavalry saber manufactured by the famous New York jewelry maker, Tiffany & Company

A children's room full of toys with trains that encourage interactive play

The famous locomotive the *General* (This story has been featured in several movies and books, most notably Buster Keaton's *The General* and Russell S. Bonds' *Stealing the General: The Great Locomotive Chase and the First Medal of Honor.*)

Spelman College Museum of Fine Art

350 Spelman Lane, SW (Map 1)
404-270-5607
www.spelman.edu/museum
Open: Tu–F, 10:00 AM–4:00 PM; Sa, noon–4:00 PM. Closed college holidays.
Admission: Free; Suggested donation, $3.00

As the only museum in the United States to specialize in works by and about women of the African diaspora, The Spelman College Museum of Fine Art is truly a national treasure. Named by the *Atlanta Journal Constitution* as one of Atlanta's "Fabulous Five Museums," the museum traces its roots to the first museum founded at Spelman College in 1899 by Reverend J. M. Lewis. With the founding of the Spelman College Art Program in the 1930s, the museum received another significant boost. Located today on the first floor of the Olivia Hanks Cosby Academic Center, the museum occupies a place of prominence on the Spelman College campus. Throughout the academic year, the Spelman College Museum of Fine Art hosts two major exhibits drawn from outside collections as well as its rich permanent collection that includes works by prominent artists from central Africa as well as accomplished African American artists. The museum's well-lit exhibition space has soaring walls and a unique flow. It is a perfect complement to the artwork on display.

Stately Oaks Plantation

100 Carriage Drive at Jodeco Road (Map 2)
Jonesboro
770-473-0197
www.historicaljonesboro.org
Open: M–F (and most Sa), 10:00 AM–4:00 PM; Tours on the hour
Admission: Adults, $12.00; Seniors, $9.00; Children 5–11, $6.00

This Greek Revival antebellum plantation was built circa 1839 and is located in historic Jonesboro. The town is known for its role in the novel *Gone with the Wind* as the location of Scarlett O'Hara's plantation home, Tara. While Tara never really existed, it is believed that the Stately Oaks Plantation represents quite closely what it would have looked like. The grounds contain the plantation home, the original log kitchen, Juddy's Country Store (souvenirs and refreshments), and the Bethel one-room schoolhouse. The house was actually used by Union soldiers during the Civil War at the Battle of Jonesboro, during which nearly the entire town was burned to the ground. Guided tours are always provided in costume, adding an extra sense of what life was truly like in the middle 1800s. We recommend calling or checking the Web site before visiting, as special events are often hosted at the plantation. These events include Civil War battle reenactments, Civil War weapon demonstrations, and period mourning rituals.

For *Gone With the Wind* enthusiasts, we recommend purchasing the Premiere Pass, which includes five separate attractions: Atlanta Cyclorama and Civil War Museum, Historical & Hysterical Tours (costumed guided car tour to various locations in Jonesboro, GA), Margaret Mitchell House, Road to Tara Museum, and Stately Oaks Plantation.

Highlights:

Costumed docents

A chair that was in the house when Sherman's troops marched on Jonesboro

The Swan House

130 West Paces Ferry Road, NW (Map 2)
404-814-4000
www.atlhist.org
Open: M–Sa, 10:00 AM–5:30 PM; Su, noon–5:30 PM
Admission: Adults, $7.00

Built in 1928, the Swan House served as the stately manor
home of Mr. and Mrs. Edward Inman, heirs to a post–Civil
War cotton brokerage fortune. Designed by noted Atlanta
architect Philip Trammell Shutze, the Swan House takes its
name from the variety of swans Shutze placed in the design
details throughout the home. The Swan House guides do an
excellent job pointing these out as visitors tour the home's
12,600 square feet and are introduced to the fashion, furnishing,
and lifestyle of Atlanta's social elite during the early 1930s and
1940s. Stops on the tour include Mr. Inman's library, the formal living room, the formal dining room, the kitchen, and the
upstairs bedrooms. Each room contains a charming combination of antiques and personal effects belonging to the Inman
family. Throughout the Swan House, much of the wallpaper
and paint is original, which means visitors must be very careful
not to touch the walls and furnishings. In 1966 the Atlanta
Historical Society purchased Swan House and its surrounding
28 acres to preserve the home exactly as Mrs. Inman requested.
In 2004 the Swan House underwent a five-million-dollar renovation. The results are truly breathtaking.

Highlights:
The floating staircase in the center of the home

Ornate, classically inspired gardens complete with fountains and sculptures

The remarkable faux marble painting in the master bathroom

The Teaching Museum North

791 Mimosa Boulevard (Map 4)

Roswell

770-552-6339

www.fultonschools.org/dept/teachingmuseumnorth

Open: M–F, 7:00 AM–3:30 PM. Due to the large number of student groups visiting the museum, the general public must call ahead to arrange a tour.

Admission: Free

The quote hanging in the Teaching Museum North says it all: "Children come here that we may teach the mind and touch the spirit." Affiliated with the Fulton County School System, the Teaching Museum North has established itself as a true Georgia gem since it opened in 1991. Its curators have worked with the National Archives, the National Holocaust Museum, and the Georgia Archives to ensure the historical accuracy of its exhibits. The museum itself is colocated with the Roswell Elementary School. Since 1840 there has been some kind of educational facility on the site. Upon entering the museum, visitors are treated to colorful and vibrant exhibits that touch on everything from local Roswell history to the presidents of the United States. Full-scale replicas of a frontier cabin and a turn-of-the-century courtroom are visitors' favorites. There is also a room dedicated to the 1930s that explores everything from the Great Depression to the Holocaust.

Highlights:

A section of the Georgia room dedicated to the state's most accomplished writers and artists

A diorama of the Roswell Mill Village

The Teaching Museum South

689 North Avenue (Map 2)

404-669-8015

www.teachingmuseumsouth.com

Open: M–F, 8:00 AM–4:30 PM. Visitors must call ahead for tour.

Admission: Free

Located in Hapeville in the former North Avenue Elementary
School, an architectural gem designed by Atlanta architect
Philip Trammel Shutze, the Teaching Museum South's motto
is "Tell me and I'll forget. Show me and I may remember.
Involve me and I'll understand." Since opening in 1992, the
museum's programs and exhibits have served 50,000 children
each year. The Teaching Museum South boasts 14 different
exhibit rooms that challenge children to consider the impact of
different events in history on the modern world. Employing a
hands-on approach to learning, the museum encourages cultural tolerance through a Native American exhibit, a "secret
annex" that recreates the tiny living space inhabited by Anne
Frank during the Holocaust, and the African Cultures exhibit.
The museum also celebrates Georgia's rich sports heritage and
its role in hosting the 1996 Summer Olympic Games.

Highlights:

The meticulously constructed exhibit rooms that authentically
capture the time periods represented

The state-of-the-art auditorium used for educational perform-
ances

The Telephone Museum

675 West Peachtree Street, NE (Map 1)
404-223-3661
www.bellsouthgapioneers.org/Museumtempnew.htm
Open: Call ahead to schedule tour; group tours encouraged.
Admission: Free

The Telephone Museum, located on the plaza level of the
BellSouth building, has interesting, well-organized exhibits
explaining the first 100 years of telecommunication history in
the United States. The museum's collection of antique wooden
phones does a wonderful job reminding visitors of what the
world was like before cell phones. The museum's first exhibit is
an interactive display highlighting the historic moment when
Alexander Graham Bell uttered his famous words: "Mr.
Watson . . . come here . . . I want to see you." Upon entering
the main exhibition space, visitors move through a series of
well-designed displays that demonstrate the early effect the
telephone had on society as well as its meteoric growth and
adoption in American households. As the tour continues, one
gets a sense of the impact of telecommunications on the world,
enabling human beings to communicate from the most remote
locations on the globe.

The Tullie Smith Farm

130 West Paces Ferry Road, NW (Map 2)
404-814-4000
www.atlhist.org
Open: M–Sa, 10:00 AM–5:30 PM; Su, noon–5:30 PM
Admission: $7.00

Located in the heart of Buckhead on the picturesque grounds of the Atlanta History Center, the Tullie Smith Farm is a spectacular collection of antebellum outbuildings that came from working farms throughout Georgia. The centerpiece of the Tullie Smith Farm is the actual farmhouse belonging to the Robert Smith family, which is on the National Register of Historic Places. Clustered around the farmhouse with a detailed description of their origin and purpose are a barn, a smokehouse, a dairy, a yeoman's cabin, a blacksmith's shop, and a corncrib. Most of these structures were originally built in the early to mid-1800s. What makes the Tullie Smith Farm unique is that it illuminates the simple, functional lifestyle led by the majority of farmers in rural Georgia. Guides are available for a walking tour of the entire farm. Visitors can stand in the door-way of most structures and see rustic period antiques, large cooking kettles, and ceramic jugs that played key roles in the daily life of Georgia's yeoman farmers. Please call ahead to see if the Atlanta History Center has scheduled any craftspeople to work the farm using techniques of the period.

Highlights:

The explanation that the purpose of dirt yards around rural farmhouses was to make it easy to detect snakes trying to slither into the house

The smokehouse with its original meat hooks

The detached kitchen used to prepare two large meals of the day for the Smith family

Williams-Payne House

6075 Sandy Springs Circle (Map 4)
Sandy Springs
404-851-9111
www.heritagesandysprings.org
Open: By appointment only; Please call.
Admission: Free

Originally located where Georgia Route 400 intersects Mount Vernon Highway, this fully restored home was built by Walter Jerome Williams in 1869. The Williams family, which included 12 children, lived off the land and grew everything from corn to sugar cane. The house deteriorated after the last Williams to occupy the house died in 1936. However, it was purchased and restored by Major and Marie Payne. The Paynes occupied the home until the early 1980s, when it was sold to investors and moved to its current location in Sandy Springs, which is surrounded by a beautifully landscaped green space. Inside the home, visitors will experience a Georgia farmhouse circa 1870. The surrounding yard contains typical extensions such as a partially underground milk house, a kitchen garden, a privy, and a gazebo. The exterior and plants are also typical of the area in that time period.

World of Coca-Cola

55 Martin Luther King, Jr., Drive (Map 1)
404-676-5151
www.worldofcocacola.com
Open: M–Sa, 9:00 AM–5:00 PM; Su, 11:00 AM–5:00 PM (Sept.–May);
M–Sa, 9:00 AM–6:00 PM; Su, 11:00 AM–5:00 PM (June–Aug.)
Admission: Adults, $9:00; Seniors, $8.00; Children 4–11, $5.00;
Children under 4, free

Created in an Atlanta pharmacy in 1886 where it was ordered
seven times a day, Coca-Cola is now sold in 200 countries
across the world, where it is ordered over a billion times a day.
The three floors of the World of Coca-Cola tell the story of
the soft drink as the world's most recognized brand through its
groundbreaking marketing and media campaigns. The tour
begins with a short film on the history of the product. It features the key Atlanta businessmen who played crucial roles in
the development and marketing of the product. After viewing
the film, visitors to the museum can stroll through an impressive collection of early Coca-Cola advertising memorabilia that
demonstrates the marketing genius of the Coca-Cola company.
Also contained on the third floor is a great film showing the
international faces of Coca-Cola. The final stops on the tour
allow visitors to get reacquainted with classic Coca-Cola commercials as well as see highlights from Coca-Cola advertising
campaigns with Santa Claus.

Highlights:
Vintage Coca-Cola commercials featuring jingles, slogans, and
celebrities that pitched the brand to American households

A pre–Civil Rights Coca-Cola advertising poster from the 1950s featuring African American track stars and gold medalists Jessie Owens and Alice Coachman

Different variations of the Coca-Cola product found around the world in the Tastes of the World section of the museum

The Wren's Nest

1050 Ralph David Abernathy Boulevard, SW (Map 1)

404-753-7735

Open: Tu–Sa, 10:00 AM–2:30 PM; Tours Tu, Th, Sa, 10:30 AM–1:30 PM on the half hour

Admission: Adults, $5.00; Children 6–12, $4.00

The Wren's Nest contains much of the original furnishings and memorabilia belonging to Joel Chandler Harris, the author of the Uncle Remus tales. Harris lived in the house from 1881 until his death in 1908. The Wren's Nest is the oldest house museum in Atlanta. It was built originally in 1870, and Harris commissioned an architect to build an addition onto the house, which survives as a beautiful one-and-a-half story cottage in the Queen Ann style. Born in Billy Barne's Tavern in 1845 to unwed Mary Harris, Joel Chandler Harris grew up in Eatonton, Georgia. The pathologically shy Harris never knew his father, and he suffered from a pronounced stutter. Somehow he befriended two elderly slaves named George Terrell and Old Harbert. They told Harris stories of Brer Rabbit and Brer Fox and other memorable characters living in the briar patch. Harris recorded the stories in the unique dialects and rhythms used in their telling. Beginning in 1880, Harris started publishing the tales, eventually getting 184 into print. Scholars have proven that more than 120 have their origins in Africa. Although remembered for the Uncle Remus tales, Harris wrote 35 books and five collections of short stories in addition to serving as editor of the *Atlanta Journal Constitution*. Designated a National Historic Landmark in 1948, the Wren's Nest takes its name from a discovery by

Harris' children: a wren had built its nest in the family mailbox in 1900. A second mailbox was immediately installed so as not to disturb the bird. The Walt Disney Company filmed some of its controversial *Song of the South*, an adaptation of the Uncle Remus tales, at Wren's Nest in 1948.

Highlights:

A bookcase filled with Harris' personal library

Photographs of the interior of the house, which are being used to restore original wallpaper and interior details

The mailbox inhabited by the famous wren in 1900

Appendix

The following lists are thematic guides to the museums located in Atlanta. All lists are in alphabetical order.

Ten Essential Museums
Atlanta Cyclorama and Civil War Museum
The Atlanta History Center
Fernbank Museum of Natural History
The High Museum of Art
Margaret Mitchell House and Museum
Martin Luther King Jr., National Historic Site
Michael C. Carlos Museum at Emory University
The Museum of the Jimmy Carter Library
Oakland Cemetery
Southern Museum of Civil War & Locomotive Museum

Only in Atlanta
Atlanta Cyclorama and Civil War Museum
Atlanta's Fox Theatre
The Braves Museum and Hall of Fame
CNN Studio Tour
Discovering Stone Mountain Museum
The Georgia Capitol Museum
The Georgia Governor's Mansion
The Herndon Home
Oakland Cemetery
The World of Coca-Cola

Ten Museums for Children

Antique Car and Treasure Museum
Center for Puppetry Arts
Imagine it! Children's Museum
The Martin Luther King, Jr., National Historic Site
The Roswell Fire and Rescue Museum
Southeastern Railway Museum
Southern Museum of Civil War & Locomotive History
The Teaching Museum North
The Teaching Museum South
The World of Coca-Cola

Ten Museums for Teenagers

Antique Car and Treasure Museum
CNN Studio Tour
The Georgia Capitol Museum
The Martin Luther King, Jr., National Historic Site
The Michael C. Carlos Museum at Emory University
The Museum of the Jimmy Carter Library
The Salvation Army Southern Historical Center and Museum
Southeastern Railway Museum
Southern Museum of Civil War & Locomotive History
The World of Coca-Cola

Ten Museums — Art and Architecture

Art Institute of Atlanta: Janet S. Day Gallery
Atlanta Contemporary Art Center
The Atlanta History Center
Clark Atlanta University Collections of African American Art
The High Museum of Art
Marietta/Cobb Museum of Art
The Museum of Contemporary Art
Museum of Design Atlanta
Oglethorpe Museum of Art
Spelman College Museum of Fine Art

Ten Museums — Civil War

Atlanta Cyclorama and Civil War Museum
The Atlanta History Center
Dekalb History Museum
Discovering Stone Mountain Museum
The Kennesaw Depot Museum
Kennesaw National Battlefield Park and Museum
Margaret Mitchell House and Museum
Marietta Museum of History
Road to Tara Museum
Southern Museum of Civil War & Locomotive History

Ten Museums — Regional Interest

Antebellum Plantation at Stone Mountain

The Atlanta History Center

Discovering Stone Mountain Museum

The Georgia Capitol Museum

The Georgia Governor's Mansion

Martin Luther King, Jr., National Historic Site

The Salvation Army Southern Historical Center and Museum

Southeastern Railway Museum

Southern Museum of Civil War & Locomotive History

The Wren's Nest

Museums — Science and Technology

Fernbank Museum of Natural History

Fernbank Science Center

The Georgia Capitol Museum

The Michael C. Carlos Museum at Emory University

Robert C. Williams American Museum of Papermaking

Southeastern Railway Museum

Southern Museum of Civil War & Locomotive History

The Telephone Museum

House Museums and Museums with Historic Houses

Antebellum Plantation at Stone Mountain

Archibald Smith Plantation Home

The Atlanta History Center

Bulloch Hall

The Georgia Governor's Mansion

The Hammonds House

The Herndon Home

The Margaret Mitchell House and Museum

The Martin Luther King, Jr., National Historic Site

Rhodes Hall: The Castle on Peachtree Street

Root House Museum

Stately Oaks Plantation

The Swan House

The Tullie Smith Farm

Williams-Payne House

The Wren's Nest

Museums that Require Appointments

Air Acres

Delta Air Transport Heritage Museum

The Herndon Home

The Salvation Army Southern Historical Center and Museum

The Telephone Museum

Index of Alternative Museum Names

The Braves Hall of Fame, see the Braves Museum and Hall of Fame

The Capitol Museum, see the Georgia Capitol Museum

The Carlos, see Michael C. Carlos Museum at Emory University

The Carter Center Museum, see the Museum of the Jimmy Carter Library

The Clark Gallery, see Clark Atlanta University Collections of African American Art

The Contemporary, see Atlanta Contemporary Art Center

The Cyclorama, see Atlanta Cyclorama and Civil War Museum

The Delta Museum, see Delta Air Transport Heritage Museum

The Fox, see Atlanta's Fox Theatre

The High, see the High Museum of Art

MLK Birth Home, see Martin Luther King, Jr., National Historic Site

MOCA, see Museum of Contemporary Art

Paper Museum, see Robert C. Williams American Museum of Papermaking

The Puppet Museum, see Center for Puppetry Arts

Spelman Gallery, see Spelman College Museum of Fine Art

Stone Mountain, see Discovering Stone Mountain Museum

About the Authors

A graduate of the University of Pennsylvania and Emory University's Goizeuta School of Business, Scott W. Hawley has climbed all 54 of the 14,000-foot mountains in Colorado. Scott and his wife Portia live in historic Kirkwood in East Atlanta.

A graduate of the Art Institute of Atlanta, Kennesaw State University, and Emory University's Goizeuta School of Business, Kevin L. Crow has toured the country as a professional singer and guitarist. Kevin, his wife Jordana, and their children Maxwell, Emerson, and Kenzie live in Smryna in Northwest Atlanta.